EQUIPPED TO SERVE

Studies in the charismata

BY KEN CHANT

EQUIPPED TO SERVE

Studies in the charismata

By Dr. Ken Chant

Copyright © 2012 Ken Chant

ISBN 978-1-61529-041-3

Vision Publishing
1672 Main St. E 109
Ramona, CA 92065
1-800-9-VISION
www.booksbyvision.com

A NOTE ON GENDER

It is unfortunate that the English language does not contain an adequate generic pronoun (especially in the singular number) that includes without bias both male and female. So *"he, him, his, man, mankind,"* with their plurals, must do the work for both sexes. Accordingly, wherever it is appropriate to do so in the following pages, please include the feminine gender in the masculine, and vice versa.

FOOTNOTES

A work once fully referenced will thereafter be noted either by "ibid" or "op. cit."

CONTENTS

ABBREVIATIONS

Abbreviations commonly used for the books of the Bible are

Genesis	Ge	Habakkuk	Hb
Exodus	Ex	Zephaniah	Zp
Leviticus	Le	Haggai	Hg
Numbers	Nu	Zechariah	Zc
Deuteronomy	De	Malachi	Mal
Joshua	Js		
Judges	Jg		
Ruth	Ru	Matthew	Mt
1 Samuel	1 Sa	Mark	Mk
2 Samuel	2 Sa	Luke	Lu
1 Kings	1 Kg	John	Jn
2 Kings	2 Kg	Acts	Ac
1 Chronicles	1 Ch	Romans	Ro
2 Chronicles	2 Ch	1 Corinthians	1 Co
Ezra	Ezr	2 Corinthians	2 Co
Nehemiah	Ne	Galatians	Ga
Esther	Es	Ephesians	Ep
Job	Jb	Philippians	Ph
Psalm	Ps	Colossians	Cl
Proverbs	Pr	1 Thessalonians	1 Th
Ecclesiastes	Ec	2 Thessalonians	2 Th
Song of Songs	Ca *	1 Timothy	1 Ti
Isaiah	Is	2 Timothy	2 Ti
Jeremiah	Je	Titus	Tit
Lamentations	La	Philemon	Phm
Ezekiel	Ez	Hebrews	He
Daniel	Da	James	Ja
Hosea	Ho	1 Peter	1 Pe
Joel	Jl	2 Peter	2 Pe
Amos	Am	1 John	1 Jn
Obadiah	Ob	2 John	2 Jn
Jonah	Jo	3 John	3 Jn
Micah	Mi	Jude	Ju
Nahum	Na	Revelation	Re

Ca is an abbreviation of *Canticles*, a derivative of the Latin name of the *Song of Solomon*, which is sometimes also called the *Song of Songs*.

"HARD WORK

AND LATE NIGHTS!"

Just over 2000 years ago an unknown Jewish author wrote a history of the miseries his people suffered under three Syrian tyrants during the second century before Christ. He opened his work with an eloquent preface that has ever since been a model for countless authors. It is such an apt description of the proper motivation for writing a book, and of the toil required that I am going to purloin it for my own preface. He complains about the mass of facts and figures that confronted him and the difficulty of compressing everything he wanted to say into one volume. But nothing daunted, he pressed bravely on -

"What a pile of statistics faced me! What a mountain of information! Yet despite the almost insuperable difficulties, I was determined to reduce it all to one book of readable history. I had three aims:

- to entertain those who read just for the pleasure of it;
- to help students who are obliged to master the facts of history; and
- to provide a work that will benefit both scholar and layman.

"Few people realise how arduous it is to achieve those aims. At the very least it demands hard work and late nights. [a]Someone who wants to put on a fine banquet and to please all the diners, must be willing to put in many hours of toil. Yet when it is all over, the host

---

[a] The translation "hard work and late nights" comes from the "Revised English Bible.

wants no better reward than the gratitude of the guests. That is just how I feel.

"My plan has been to stick to the main points of my theme, and not get tangled in too much detail. I am like an architect who designs the general shape of a new building, then leaves it to others to pay attention to particulars of structure and decoration. It may be the duty of an original historian to tell everything there is to know about everything that happened, but that is not my task. My goal is more simple: not to spread myself across the whole terrain, but to be concise, and to show the main events and what they mean for my readers. So then, without further ado, let me get on with the story. It would be silly to stretch out this preface while cutting short the actual history!"[a]

The book you are now holding at least partly reflects the example of the ancient historian: it cost me "hard work and late nights". I am less confident about the loftier aims of pleasant reading, sound instruction, and general benefit. Judgment on those matters must be left, dear reader, to you. But I may hope at least that nothing in these pages contradicts sound doctrine, and that the end result will be a company of people fully equipped to serve Christ through the remarkable power of the charismata the Holy Spirit has planted in the church.

---

[a] 2 Maccabees 2:23-32

WHAT A WOMAN!

St Augustine of Hippo, in his great work *The City of God*, scornfully contrasts with the true and amazing miracles that occur in the church, the lying wonders performed by demons. Nonetheless, he does not doubt that demons, by their own "force and power", do enable their devotees to perform prodigious feats. Thus he describes a number of "miracles", which he says that "history vouches for", such as -

- ◆ Aeneas brought from Troy to Rome a collection of household gods called the Penates, which had the power to move themselves from one place to another;
- ◆ Tarquinius, an early king of Rome (circa 500 B.C.), established his royal authority by cutting a grindstone with a knife as if it were butter;
- ◆ a deadly serpent travelled with the physician Asclepius (who later became a god) on a journey from Epidaurus in Greece to Rome;
- ◆ a Vestal Virgin, accused of immoral conduct, proved her innocence by filling a sieve with water and carrying it from one place to another without losing a drop.

But the finest of all the exploits occurred when a large ship conveying to Rome the sacred image of a goddess hit a mud bank and was stuck fast. The vessel resisted all attempts by men, oxen, and machines to move it. Along came a virtuous maiden who tied her girdle to it, pulled it free, and hauled it down the river with ease! [a] What a woman! She proved the invincibility of chastity and became a model that Greek and Roman matrons thereafter held admonishingly before their daughters.

---

[a] Book X, Chapter 16.

Elsewhere, Augustine describes other wonders and supernatural events that were performed in the temples of the pagans. Some of them were mere trickery, like the iron image that floated in mid-air, suspended between two pieces of hidden loadstone. The gullible were persuaded that it was a miracle.[a] Others were more subtle, resulting from the skill of demons who were "able to enhance the works of the magicians to such a level of power" that they were seemingly able to "stop rivers from flowing, make the stars move in a different direction, call out ghosts from the grave at midnight, compel trees to uproot and walk along the ground, and to shake the very earth itself."[b]

Against those phenomena spawned in hell Augustine set the greater and gracious gifts of God - miracles that were designed not to astound but to heal, not to amaze but deliver, not to induce grovelling servitude but to produce free sons and daughters of God. What is the source of those divinely wrought signs and wonders? Paul says that they stem from the *"charismata"*, the gifts of the Holy Spirit that have been set in the church by God. By those gifts Spirit-filled Christians are equipped to serve the Lord, and the church is enabled to be what Jesus himself would be if he were here in person. What *would* he do? He would heal the sick, deliver the oppressed, set the prisoners free, speak the oracles of God, and build the church. By the *charismata* we can do the same.

[a] Book XXI, Chapter 6

[b] Ibid

Chapter One

GOD SPEAKS!

"Now concerning spiritual gifts, my friends, I do not want you to be ignorant."

With that blunt sentence, Paul begins a discourse on the *charismata*[a] - that is, the supernatural gifts of the Holy Spirit that were part of the life and worship of the early church (1 Co 12:7-11). Paul here mentions nine of them, and in the familiar words and order of the KJV, they are:

- a word of wisdom
- a word of knowledge
- the gift of faith
- gifts of healing
- working of miracles
- prophecy
- discerning of spirits
- the gift of tongues
- interpretation of tongues

The Corinthians, it seems, lacked proper information about these gifts, and were therefore running into problems. So Paul wrote to combat their ignorance, and to show them (and us) how the charismata should function within a local church.

The strife at Corinth did not come from uncertainty about the *existence* of the charismata. On the contrary, the Corinthians were

---

[a] The name comes from the Greek word Paul uses to describe the special gifts ("charismata") of the Holy Spirit in the church.

overly aware of the gifts and too exuberant in their use of them. Paul saw an urgent need to correct that abuse of sacred privilege. But to avoid any risk of his readers misunderstanding him and of accusing him of scorning the charismata, he decided first to stress their special value.

What is that value?

They provide the church with access to an extraordinary dimension of worship and ministry. Paul highlights this in a striking way:

- ◆ he begins by contrasting their new supernatural potential in Christ with the characteristics of their old pagan life;
- ◆ then he shows them how to tell true charismata from those that are false;
- ◆ then he provides a list of various spiritual gifts, comments on the way they are distributed around the church, and gives a set of rules to govern their use in the church.

I. LIVING AMONG MIRACLES

Paul's opening words were "Now, concerning spiritual gifts..." The phrase "spiritual gifts" is a translation of the Greek word *"pneumatika"*, which means literally "spiritualities". It can be given either a *neuter* or *masculine* sense:

- ◆ if **neuter**, it means "spiritual matters, experiences, or things"; or (because of the context, vs. 8-10) "spiritual gifts";
- ◆ if **masculine**, it means "spiritual persons", or "people with spiritual gifts".

If Paul is talking about *people*, then his opening statement may be linked with his reference to those who *"speak by the Spirit of God"* (vs. 3), which includes speaking in tongues (cp. the synonymous expressions in 14:2,14). Apparently (14:39) some of the people in the church at Corinth were fearful of glossolalia, and were trying to prevent it. Perhaps they thought it might be blasphemous. But Paul assures them that anyone who speaks in tongues in response to an infilling of the Holy Spirit will be praising Christ, not cursing him. He had no doubt about the devout nature of Christian glossolalia.

However, if he is talking about *things*, then this opening statement may be linked with his comments about the charismata in general. In that case, Paul's counsel must be applied to every kind of spiritual manifestation in the church.

Either way, we gain at the outset a vision of the real calling of the church: we should live freely in a realm that remains unknown to unbelievers, a spiritual realm, a supernatural realm, where the ordinary rules and limitations of nature no longer hold supremacy. This is a dimension where the transcendent becomes normal, where answered prayer is taken for granted, where miracles are commonly expected, where divine supply and heavenly strength are always anticipated. It is a level of life where the believer dwells in conscious union with heaven, where, in fact, *"as God is, so are we in this present world"* (1 Jn 4:17b). Here we can live as Jesus did, drawing continually upon all the resources of the Father.

Now, this spiritual realm exists, and every believer is invited to step out of the confines of ordinary earth-bound living, and to step up, and into, *"the heavenlies"* (Ep 1:3; 2:6; etc) where divine riches abound.

The early church, generally speaking, did live in that dimension. Initially they were excited and amazed at the miracles that occurred in their ministry (Lu 10:17); but later, in *Acts* and in the *Letters*, there are many accounts of marvellous signs, wonders, and miracles, told almost casually, without ado. The early Christians accepted that living among miracles was the ordinary pattern for the church. As Donald Gee said, "it was among the outsiders that the excitement occurred"; but for the Christians, frequent experience of the miraculous was normal.

Why is this no longer so in many churches? Simply because the people of God have chosen to ignore this spiritual realm. Is that really possible? Yes, because we are tri-partite creatures, possessing a body, a soul, and a spirit. [a]Therefore, there are three levels on which Christians can live: the physical; the soulish; or the spiritual. Your *body* gives you contact with the world around you; your *soul* enables you to have understanding of yourself and of your neighbour; and your *spirit* gives you access to God. The *body* deals with physical and material things. The *soul* deals with your thoughts and emotions, and with your consciousness of beauty or ugliness, of good or evil, and so on. *The spirit* reaches into the realm of God and touches on heavenly things and divine forces.

So then, we must all choose whether we will normally live on the level of the -

(A) PHYSICAL, PSYCHICAL, OR SPIRITUAL

Which one have you chosen? Do you live -

- ♦ *on the level of the body*, governed only by physical appetite and desire, which the Bible calls "living in the flesh"; or

- ♦ *on the level of the soul*, never rising any higher than your own thoughts, feelings, emotions, or sensibilities, which the Bible calls living "by sight" or "by feeling"; or
- ♦ *in the realm of the Spirit*, dwelling in the life and power of a revelation from God?

To put it another way, some people are dominated by their *flesh* and its appetites; some people are dominated by their *soul,* driven by their feelings, limited by what they can see, hear, or understand by

---

[a] I am aware of the alternative bi-partite view, that we have only a body and a soul/spirit; and there are other theories also. But for the purpose of the argument above it is convenient to separate soul and spirit.

themselves; while others are dominated by the *spirit*, and so are able to draw upon all the resources of heaven.

(B) WORSHIPPING GOD WITH POWER

This principle applies to worship as well as to any other part of life. It is what Jesus meant when he said that we must worship God in spirit. Worship is valueless if it exists *only* on the level of the flesh, or of the soul. We must worship God on the level of the spirit. But the worship of many people never rises above the flesh. That is, they go to church out of mere habit, or because it is expected of them, or because they are compelled, or because they think it is the right thing to do. Neither their soul (their emotions), nor their spirit, are ever touched by their worship.

Then there are others who do bring their soul into the act of worship, but they seldom rise into true spiritual worship. They depend on a beautiful building, on gorgeous ritual, and on the majesty of organ, choir, and ceremony. Such things - such outward show and atmosphere - have an aesthetic appeal to the soul. They catch the attention of the eye and ear; they stir the feelings and the emotions; but they do not, of themselves, lead to a truly spiritual worship.

I do not mean to condemn the use of aesthetic appeal. The gorgeous liturgy of Israel's ancient Temple, the magnificent ritual that God himself instituted, show that every form of human artistry can be used for the glory of God. But it can happen - as it did with Israel - that people rest on the level of soulish appeal and advance no further. Then their worship may be in vain. They may honour God with their ceremonial while their hearts are far from him (Mt 15:8-9).

On the other hand, when people have learned how to worship God in spirit their circumstances become irrelevant to the effectiveness of their worship. If they are free to do so, they may well choose to augment their worship, and to encounter God, through every device of liturgical art; but, if the appurtenances of ceremony are stolen, if they are restricted to a barren place, with only themselves and God, their worship will still be rich and glorious. Perhaps it is the difference between "praying" and "saying prayers", or between "worship" and merely doing "acts of worship".

When people enter a truly spiritual dimension of worship they can begin to enjoy access to a continuous heavenly supply. It is in this realm that the *charismata* are designed to operate. It is by the presence of the charismata in worship that the supernatural becomes natural and the church revels in the unlimited resources of God.

II. NEW WORSHIP OR OLD PAGANISM?

See 1 Co 12:2-3. Paul develops two ideas here. On the one hand, he insists that the idols of the heathen were dumb. On the other, he allows that supernatural phenomena were found in pagan rites. So we find two contrasts -

(A) THE LIVING GOD VERSUS DUMB IDOLS

Before they had come to know the true God, the Corinthians had been idolaters. They had worshipped stone gods; and as the psalmist had said (Ps 135:15-18), worshipping idols that were dumb they made themselves dumb. Since the idol could not speak, neither could it impel speech in any of its devotees. But we have come to the living God, who speaks himself, and is also able to implant words of revelation, prophecy, praise, and prayer, on the lips of his servants. Our God is not silent! By placing the charismata in the church the Holy Spirit has created a channel through which the divine presence may be continually manifested, and among the people of God the voice of heaven may be continually heard.

(B) TRUE VOICES VERSUS THE SPURIOUS

(1) *While the idols of the heathen were dumb, it was still true* that many pagan priests were able to deliver oracles, and they could perform seemingly prodigious feats (cp. Ac 8:9-11; 13:6,8-10; Ex

7:10-12,20-22; 8:6-7; etc). These pagan "signs" often involved plain chicanery. Judicious use of pulleys and levers, secret chambers, ventriloquism, and other unscrupulous and cunning devices, were enough to dupe a gullible and superstitious public. Yet there were also counterfeit wonders, stemming from demonic influence, which were therefore truly supernatural (or at least preternatural), but nonetheless false. That being so, Paul gave two tests by which the spirit behind a prophet or oracle could be recognised –

(a) *No one who disowned Christ, or who by word or behaviour blasphemed Christ, could be acting under the influence of the Spirit of God. The church should not allow itself to be deceived by the seeming supernatural quality of such oracles, nor by any other apparent miracle (cp. De 13:1-3). If the end result of some "pneumatikon" was to cast reproach on Christ, it had to be strictly rejected.*

(b) *No one could claim Christ as Lord, and so live and speak as to induce others also to acknowledge his authority, except by the Holy Spirit. If an oracle or a "sign" agrees with scripture and brings glory to the Son of God, then the church may pronounce it activated by the Spirit of God. The faith that recognises Christ as Saviour and Lord is a faith that can be inwrought by the Holy Spirit alone.*

(2) *The reason for Paul's exhortation appears to be this:* apart from permitting a disorderly exercise of the genuine gifts of the Spirit, the Corinthians were also allowing spurious gifts to occur in their meetings. Perhaps they were fearful of quenching any "prophet" who seemed to be divinely inspired. But Paul warned them: just as they had once been led astray by idolatry, and had blindly followed the trickery and demonic falsehoods of their pagan priests, so now they were being led astray again. He urged them to correct the wrong use of genuine spiritual gifts, and to reject those gifts that were false. The same warning is repeated (though in different terms) in Ep 4:14, and in 1 Jn 4:1-3. See also Mt 7:14,16,21-23 (cp. Ac 19:13-16); 24:11; 2 Jn 7; Re 2:2; De 18:20-22; 1 Th 5:19-22).

(3) John said that we should *"test the spirits"* by applying this criterion: *"every spirit that confesses that Jesus Christ has come in the flesh is of God."* This "test", or course, demands more than a mere repetition of words. To serve his own ambitions Satan would no doubt be willing to quote the whole Bible from end to end! *"Confessing that Jesus Christ has come in the flesh"* requires a living demonstration of deep belief that Jesus is the incarnate Christ, so that every word and act displays recognition of his absolute lordship. That kind of "confession" is impossible for false spirits. There are people who claim to have spiritual gifts and a revelation from God; they glibly speak the name of Jesus; but doctrines contrary to the gospel, a life barren of the fruit of the Spirit, a witness inconsistent with the lordship of Christ, even the practise of immorality in the name of God, all loudly declare that they are motivated by something other than the Holy Spirit.

(4) Note that the charismata are given by the Spirit of God for exercise in the church, which is the "body" of Christ. If a person insists on moving outside the influence and authority of the church, refusing to accept oversight or discipline, his claims of special spirituality, or revelation, or doctrine, or power, should be rejected. So also should the claims of any person who seeks to use the charismata for personal gain rather than *to "edify the church"* (1 Co 14:12; Ac 8:18-24). Peter writes

> *"Since you have all received something from God, <u>use your gifts to help each other</u>. You will then be good stewards of God. Are you a speaker? Then talk like someone who is delivering an oracle from God! Are you called to serve? Then do it in the strength that God himself supplies. In everything make sure that God is glorified through Jesus Christ, for to him alone belong glory and dominion forever and ever. Amen!" (1 Pe 4:10-11).*

The true exercise of spiritual gifts will always produce an echo of Peter's joyous praise: *"To him belong glory and dominion for ever and ever. Amen!"*

ADDENDUM

"SLAIN IN THE SPIRIT"

I am opposed to any kind of cataleptic or robotic practice in the church. Religious hysteria should have no place in Christian piety. Why? Because there has already been a time in my life when a strong man held me in his grip and forced me to do his will (Lu 11:21-22). That was when I was a slave to sin and death, under the mastery of Satan, unable to shake off his chains.

But then I met Christ.

He did as the gospel promised: he set me free, lifted me up upon my feet, restored to me my lost dignity, and gave me back my liberty. Now he has invited me into partnership with him in building the kingdom as a freeborn son of God. How then could I suppose that he wants to reduce me again to a state of mindless automatism, to rob me of self-awareness and self-control?

Yet that is just what many Christians do seem to hunger for. They eagerly pursue some kind of religious prostration, under the guise of being "slain in the Spirit" or "falling under the power", as if such experiences were unmistakably acts of God. Preachers who can produce such effects in their hearers are deemed highly gifted and full of the Holy Ghost. Now those ministers may indeed be mighty in the Lord, but if they are, it has nothing to do with causing people to tumble to the floor, or shake or tremble, or any other such thing.

Do I mean that no one in the church should ever fall down before the Lord? Of course not! But there is a vast difference between a willing human response to the awesome presence of God (of which there are several scriptural examples), and the idea that God (unless he is executing judgment) demonstrates his presence by forcibly prostrating men and women. Must I suppose that the Father has suddenly become like one of those ancient oriental tyrants who required supplicants to fall face down before their thrones? In scripture, the only people who were prostrated by an act of God were victims of some divine judgment.

Surely Christ came to lift us up, to restore our ruined nobility, to cause us to stand tall and to enter boldly into the presence of God (He 10:19-23)? Jesus did not throw people onto the ground when they came to him - only the demons did that (Lu 4:35; 9:39,42; Mk 1:26; etc). The biblical proposition is better expressed in the oracle of Ezekiel -

> *"The Lord said to me, 'Son of man, stand up on your feet so that I can speak with you!' While he was speaking, the Spirit came into me and stood me on my feet" (2:1-2).*

(A) DISCERN RIGHT FROM WRONG

Once again, I do not mean it is always wrong for people to prostrate themselves before the Lord, nor that they should not expect to fall to the ground if they feel the touch of God. The Lord is always willing to meet us at the point of faith.

But it is certainly wrong to teach that such prostrations are normally caused by a direct act of God, or that they are necessarily a sign of his presence and power. Encouraging people to locate the presence of the Lord in a religious experience (especially one with no firm biblical warrant), rather than in scripture, is perilous.

You should realise too that such experiences as religious prostration are common to all faiths; there are none that are uniquely Christian. Therefore they cannot in themselves prove anything about the nearness of God. Remember again Paul's reference to *pneumatika* in 1 Co 12:1. As we have seen, the word describes any kind of religious or spiritual experience, including various spiritual leaders, gurus, and the like, both Christian and pagan. Paul wanted the Corinthians to learn how to distinguish between the true and the false. Why? Because many of the phenomena that occurred in the churches could also be found in the pagan temples, and many of the pagan prophets could produce miracles akin to those of Christian ministers (cp. Ac 8:9-11).

Those similarities can still confuse even Christian leaders, so that they unwisely allow themselves to become caught up in the excitement of supernatural phenomena. But not everything that looks like a miracle is a work of the Holy Spirit; it may instead be merely psychic, or even demonic.

(B) WHERE IS THE POWER?

Many people who depend upon a non-biblical experience such as prostration find only disappointment; that is, they are not changed nor helped by the experience. For example, they fall to the floor sick, and they stand up again, still sick. Was God then really the direct cause of their prostration? Does he mock his own dear children? Will you accuse him of using his power merely to play a game, knocking people to the floor, yet not giving them what they most want and need?

Further, if people have been taught that their prostration was a direct act of divine power, yet they are not healed, then they are brought to the end of their hope and faith. They are left with nowhere else to go; they are locked into a spiritual dead end, for if a specific surge of divine energy cannot heal them, what is there left to hope for?

To say that God "slays" people by his own hand, but then does not heal them, surely makes him a pitiless tyrant. Is he just a bully, cruelly toying with the lives and hopes of his servants, treating them like mere things, like pawns in some crass game? I cannot believe that the Father so deals with any of his beloved.

(C) WELCOME THE GENUINE

Genuine spiritual experiences (including prostration) may be welcomed and enjoyed; but they should be called human responses to the presence of God, rather than direct actions of God. What shall we say then to those ministers who insist that it really is the power of God at work when they lay hands on people, causing them to be "slain in the Spirit"? Two things -

(1) No doubt many of those ministers really are powerful in God, and are certainly his agents, bringing the lost to Christ, healing the sick, casting out demons, and the like. I have no mandate to judge or condemn the servants of God. But I may and will call into question practices that have no scriptural warrant, or claims that have no biblical foundation - especially when they seem to me to oppose some of the most fundamental truths of the gospel.

(2) It is easy to create an environment where such experiences as religious prostration happen (indeed, where they become all but irresistible), which shows plainly enough that they have a lot more to do with human action and response than with the power of God.

(a) History tells us that religious prostrations have frequently appeared in conjunction with the ministry of various evangelists and mystics. Such happenings were often welcomed initially, but later discarded when it was realised that they did more harm than good.

For example, on the fits and convulsions that initially accompanied his and Whitefield's meetings, and that were interpreted by the faithful as signs of the presence of the Holy Spirit, John Wesley held a sceptical opinion. I have read somewhere that he ordered buckets of water to be thrown over people whose cataleptic behaviour became too disruptive. He realised that the effectiveness of the revival would be harmed if he allowed such things to continue. He knew that many sober-thinking and responsible people would be repelled by such behaviour.

Because of such wisdom, Wesley's ministry continued with unabated power.

One consequence was that England was saved the awful revolution that a few decades later tore fair France apart with blood and terror. Instead of revolution, Great Britain enjoyed a mighty spiritual revival! Had Wesley not been so wise, who knows what the outcome might have been?[a]

   (b) Nowadays you can go into churches where every person who is prayed for falls to the ground, and into others where no one falls. I have ministered in both environments. I have called a prayer line in churches where every body is expected to "fall under the power" when hands were laid on them, and so they all fell. Then I have called the same kind of prayer line in other churches where no one is expected to fall, and so they all stood on their feet.

---

[a] It is also noteworthy that religious prostrations, and other such seizures, were formerly associated, not with <u>blessing</u>, but with deep conviction of <u>sin</u>! Thus Spurgeon ("Treasury of David", on Ps 6:6-7): "May not this explain some of the convulsions and hysterical attacks which have been experienced under convictions in the revivals in Ireland? Is it surprising that some should be smitten to the earth, and begin to cry aloud, when we find that David himself made his bed to swim, and grew old while he was under the heavy hand of God?"

The differences between those earlier prostrations and some modern versions of the same experiences probably arise from cultural and/or environmental conditioning, from peer group examples, and the like. On the whole, crowds will behave as they have been taught to behave, whether consciously or unconsciously, and the psychological pressure can become almost irresistible, both upon those who have had no previous knowledge of the phenomenon and upon those who try to resist it.

Am I then full of power in one place, but void of it in another? Hardly. Whether or not people fell down when hands are laid on them has far more to do with their own expectations than it does with any action of the Holy Spirit.

(c) I have also observed that in either environment (falling or standing) there is no difference in what the people receive from God. About the same percentage in each case are healed, or gain an answer to their prayer; and about the same percentage go away disappointed. Surely it is plain enough that God may be no more present when people are tumbling like autumn leaves than when they remain quietly on their feet.

(3) To summarise then: from time to time such experiences as religious prostration crop up in the church, and are given an identity and a definition –

(a) In our time physical collapse is being described by such terms as *"slain in the Spirit"*, and many assume that it results from a direct act of the Holy Spirit; it is said to be a work of divine power

(b) Whenever you encounter such defined experiences, especially if in some way they are, or seem to be, antagonistic to the gospel, then you must either: reject the **experience** as spurious; or change the **definition** so that it conforms to scripture (as I have tried to do above). In the case of a *compulsive* or *involuntary* experience (such as some forms of prostration), the following explanations are possible:

- It is an extraordinary act of God, wrought for some special purpose of grace or of judgement; or
- It is demonic in it's source and control; or
- It is a quirk of human religious nature; that is, it is a common reaction to a particular religious or spiritual stimulus; or
- It is an amalgram of several of the above.

"All that glitters is not gold," says the proverb. Not every *"pneumatikon"* should be embraced as genuine, says Paul. Be sober, discriminating, careful, before you leap to attribute some spiritual or religious phenomenon to an act of God. Not everything that looks supernatural comes from heaven. [a]

---

[a] The comments in the above Addendum, of course, can be applied, not just to religious prostrations but also to other phenomena, such as "holy laughter:, "levitations", and so on. Seldom should such manifestations be attributed to the Holy Spirit.

Chapter Two

NINE FROM HEAVEN

See 1 Co 12:7-11. The Holy Spirit has an infinite number of ways to work through his people, and he equips them with many extraordinary powers to fulfil their appointed tasks. Who could ever list all the heavenly skills that the Lord expresses through the church? Paul mentions the great *"variety of gifts"* that are available, but is content to describe just nine of them. Others are mentioned elsewhere in the New Testament, but these nine are perhaps either more prominent or more necessary to the work of the church.

For convenience, we may classify the nine gifts as follows (once again using the familiar terminology of the KJV) -

GIFTS OF REVELATION

- the word of wisdom
- the word of knowledge
- the discerning of spirits

GIFTS OF POWER

- the gift of faith
- the gifts of healing
- the working of miracles

GIFTS OF UTTERANCE

- the gift of prophecy
- the gift of tongues
- interpretation of tongues

I. THE GIFTS OF REVELATION

(A) THE WORD OF WISDOM

This gift is placed first in Paul's list. Why? Probably because of its supreme importance. Here is one gift we should certainly *"covet earnestly"* (1 Co 12:31; and cp. Pr 3:13; 4:7; 16:16).

It is only a *"word"* of wisdom. The recipient is not made perennially wise, like Solomon. Rather, this gift is an imparted fragment of the measureless resources of divine wisdom, given to meet a special need.

It is not a permanent gift. One does not receive from it an unfailing fount of wisdom at all times and in all circumstances. Some Christians may have this gift operating more frequently or more consistently than others; nonetheless, each time it is used it is a new flash of divine wisdom, a quick revelation, a "word" from the Spirit, given in response to faith for the benefit of some part of the church.

Wisdom may be defined as *the proper application of knowledge*. This spiritual gift then, makes divine insight available to confound critics, to sort out tangled situations, to put together assorted facts, and so on. This is not natural or human wisdom; it is a portion of heavenly wisdom given to solve a problem that lies beyond the resources of ordinary understanding. Nor should this gift be confused with natural insight, nor with teaching ability. Remember that it is fragmentary, and supernatural, revealed to a believer by the inspiration of the Holy Spirit to meet a specific need.

The gift operates in the following circumstances -

(1) *In preaching*: how much this gift is needed for effective preaching of the Word of God! It surely operated in the preaching of the apostles. It may function both in the interpretation of Scripture and in the selection of topic and material to be presented (1 Co 2:1; 6-7; Ac 4:13; 6:10).

(2) *In apostolic ministry*: how often the leaders of the early church needed a word of divine wisdom as they directed the affairs of the church (Ac 15:28). And it is no less needed today by those who are called to exercise an apostolic ministry and oversight in the work of God.

(3) *In pastoral ministry*: there is no gift more precious than this to any good shepherd who cares about the personal needs and problems of the flock (cp. 1 Co 7:25, 40b; 2 Pe 3:15).

(4) *In business matters*: those who are chosen to guide the business affairs of the church surely realise their need for an impartation of the acumen of heaven. One of the qualifications for the first seven chosen for such work was that they be *"full of the Holy Spirit and wisdom"* (Ac 6:3).

(5) *In emergencies*: in any activity in which a believer finds himself or herself engaged, how wonderful to know that there is always the possibility of receiving from God a *"word of wisdom"* to dispel confusion, resolve uncertainty, and reveal the solution. By this gift also, the Lord can give warning of danger and instruction in the way to safety (cp. Ac 23:7).

(6) *In service for God*: by the operation of this gift, God can reveal the task he has chosen for each person, directing us to fulfil his purpose, revealing how his work can be accomplished (cp. Ac 13:2; 16:6,7; Ga 2:1-2).

(7) *In personal guidance*: when circumstances face you that leave you bewildered, not knowing which way to turn, or what is the right answer, this gift can show the choice that will prosper under God's blessing (cp. Ja 1:5-6).

(8) *In defence of the truth*: when called upon to given sudden witness of the truth, to testify about Christ before the ungodly,

there is a promise of divine wisdom (Lu 21:14-15; and cp. Stephen, Ac 7:54).

The great importance of this gift is shown by the lament of Christ (Lu 16:8). The Master recognised that the people of this world, living in the worldly sphere, draw eagerly upon all their sources of wisdom in an effort to prosper their affairs. But he sadly observed that the saints, who are called to live in the realm of the Spirit, often fail to seek that *"wisdom that comes from above"*, which alone can enable them to accomplish all their undertakings successfully.

(B) THE WORD OF KNOWLEDGE

This gift is closely related to the former, for God's *wisdom* is based on his perfect *knowledge* of all things. The Holy Spirit has the task of taking a fragment of that all-knowingness and of conveying it to the believer, as each occasion requires.

This is not knowledge gained by learning, nor information received from any human source. It is rather the Holy Spirit imparting a fragment (a *"word"*) of divine knowledge concerning anything in heaven or on earth. It may be information that could not be gained in any other way; or it may be knowledge that the Lord chooses to give apart from the usual channels. Paul links both of these revelatory gifts of wisdom and knowledge with prayer and the supernatural influence of the Holy Spirit (Ep 1:17). That is, without prayer, and without a Spirit-controlled life, these two gifts of revelation are unlikely to flourish.

The gift operates in the following circumstances:

(1) *In teaching ministry*: undoubtedly, those called upon to teach the word of God will have great need of this endowment to lift them beyond purely natural resources in their knowledge of scripture and of the needs of the people. Donald Gee has made the important suggestion that this gift may in fact find its predominant

exercise through the teaching ministries Christ has set in the Church.

(2) *Revelation of events*: giving knowledge of happenings that concern the person whom receives the gift:

-cp. Jn 1:48; 4:18; 11:14; Ac 9:10-12; 10:4-6, 19-20; 27:21-26.

(3) *Revelation of facts*: giving information about persons, places, events, that is needed by someone to enable him or her to fulfil the purpose of God. This knowledge may also be revealed simply as a sign to lead a person to repentance and faith (cp. Jesus and the woman at the well; also Jn 4:52-53; Lu 5:4-8; Jn 21:5-6).

(4) *Revelation of truth*: giving sudden understanding of the true nature of a person, object, or anything else (cp. Mt 16:16). It also involves an apprehension of the truth of the scripture that goes beyond ordinary thought and study (Lu 21:14-15; 12:11-12).

(5) *Revelation of judgment*: see Ac 5:1-11.

The expression *"word"* of knowledge does not require a *spoken* communication. It means no more than an inner revelation to the recipient of part of God's knowledge. It is knowledge flashed onto the consciousness of that person so that, without inquiry or reasoning, he or she simply *knows* the truth about a matter. This revelation may be entirely private, intended for only the recipient. At other times it may be necessary to pass the information on to someone else.

(C) THE DISCERNING OF SPIRITS

This is not the gift of critical appraisal of other people; it does not enable the recipient to analyse the motives and character of others; it is not a cover for curiosity, nor a license to criticise. In other words, it is not the gift of "discerning of men"; it is the gift of *"discerning of spirits"*.

The uses of this gift are -

(1) *In the ministry of deliverance*: to determine if a person is suffering from a physical affliction, or from a complaint that has a spiritual origin. If the person's trouble has a demonic source, then this gift can enable the minister to determine the nature, and perhaps also the number of such demons (cp. Lu 13:10-16; Mk 5:8-13; Ac 16:16-18; 13:10-12).

(2) *In recognising false prophets*: see Ac 13:9-10; 16:16-18 and cp. 1 Ti 4:1; 2 Pe 2:1-2; Mt 24:24; 2 Co 11:13-15.

(3) *In assessing spiritual gifts*: showing if someone is speaking or acting from the natural mind or under the impulse of the Holy Spirit (1 Co 14:29).

So this gift may operate to reveal the activity of either the Holy Spirit or Satan. It can show whether or not a spiritual power is present, and, if one is present, whether it is of the devil or from God.

II. THE GIFTS OF POWER

(A) FAITH

"Faith" considered as a gift of the Holy Spirit must not be confused with the more general kind of faith frequently mentioned in scripture.

The *gift* of faith is not saving faith. Nor is it merely faith in God's Word. Nor is it the common quality of trust in God that all Christians must have.

The *gift* of faith is a special manifestation of the Holy Spirit, one that is just as supernatural as the other charismata. It is a divine implanting of the *"faith of God"*, irresistible, all-powerful, into the heart of a believer. It is given to meet a need for which the only solution is a miracle.

Something of the nature of this faith appears in the story of Joshua commanding the sun to stand still, or of Elijah binding and loosing the waters of the heavens, or of Isaiah moving the shadow back ten degrees. Jesus must have had this gift in mind when he said that believers, if they had *"the faith of God"* (Mk 11:22, lit.) could *"move a mountain"* with a word of command (cp. also 1 Co 13:2).

This faith may be given to a trusting child of God to meet a deep crisis, or to enable him or her to take advantage of a rich opportunity. It brings triumphant certainty, a confidence that brooks no barrier, conquers every difficulty, and makes the impossible almost absurdly easy.

(B) GIFTS OF HEALING

This gift (in the Greek text) is described by a double plural: *"gifts of healings"*, which suggests –

(1) Every time a person is healed by God in answer to prayer this is a gift in itself, a specific work of the Holy Spirit. It hints that divine healing occurs only in response to a definite prompting or act of the Holy Spirit. That is why the Spirit-filled Christian cannot walk into, say, a hospital, and pray indiscriminately for all the sick who are lying there. We must wait for the direction of the Holy Spirit. We may pray, but there can be no healing unless it is given by the Spirit (cp. Jn 5:1-9, where Jesus healed only one man and ignored the remaining *"multitude of invalids, blind, lame, paralysed"*; also see Ja 5:13-16, where the healing promise is associated with certain conditions, as it is also in 1 Co 11:30).

(2) There are different forms of the healing ministry - various persons may be especially used by God to pray for specific afflictions - e.g. demon possession, cancer, deafness, etc. There is no biblical evidence that I am aware of for such "specialisation" in a healing ministry, but there are indications of it happening in contemporary practice. Opinions will differ on whether or not it is wise for anyone to focus their ministry so narrowly.

Perhaps both of the above suggestions contain an element of truth. Certainly we can affirm that the person through whom the gift is manifested is merely an agent of God, and that each particular work of healing must be a direct act of the Holy Spirit.

(3) The biblical *gift of healing* cannot be limited to an exercise of medical science. This is a supernatural manifestation of the Holy Spirit, imparted quite independently of human skill. Nor is this gift an exercise of mind-over-matter, or auto-suggestion, or positive-thinking, or any other mental phenomenon. It is dependent upon simple faith in God. Nor is it a permanent power given to any one person to heal all sick people; rather it is set in the "body" of Christ to equip Christians for the service of God, and to enable them to appropriate the benefits of the healing covenant God has made with his people (cp. Ac 8:6-7; 28:8-10; etc).

(4) Paul's contention that only some Christians have the gifts of healing (1 Co 12:30) may show that this gift is a ministry given to chosen individuals; that is, some people are specially called by God to bring his healing power to the sick. If that is so, then the *gifts of healing* must be distinguished from the *healing commission* that has been given to the church in general and to elders in particular. Christ said that all believers have the privilege of laying hands on the sick, and to heal them in his name (Mk 16:16-17). And James instructed the elders of the church to pray for the healing of those who call upon them (Ja 5:14-15). However, perhaps those two latter cases function mainly within the confines of the church; while in the former case, a person endowed with definite gifts of healing should fulfil his or her ministry in the wider sphere of the world (cp. Ac 5:12-16; 8:5-8; 19:11-12; etc).

(C) THE WORKING OF MIRACLES

The Greek phrase may be translated as *"operations of divine power -* that is, mighty *works*, rather than mere revelation, or inspiration, as in other gifts of the Spirit.

Concerning this gift of power, note -

(1) MIRACLES INCLUDE PHYSICAL HEALING

There are some outstanding healings that obviously come within the scope of this spectacular gift of the Holy Spirit, such as a creative miracle, when a missing organ is replaced in the body. Hence this gift could include the recreation of an eardrum, growth of a withered hand, restoring sight to a person born blind, and other phenomena that are contrary to the process of nature. "Healing", in the ordinary sense, means a cure, or recovery, which begins with an act of God, but then, once the progress has begun, proceeds more or less naturally. *Instantaneous* recovery would involve the working of a miracle rather than merely initiating a process of healing.

(2) THIS GIFT IS NOT CONFINED TO HEALING

The working of miracles embraces a wider field than physical healing. It may include healing, but also goes far beyond it. For example, both a work of healing, and the working of a miracle are suggested in the account of the ten lepers (Mt 17:12-19). All ten lepers were *"cleansed"*, (or healed of the disease); but the one who returned and worshipped Christ was *"made whole"* - that is, fully restored, so that he was left without a trace of leprosy or of its scars anywhere in his body.

(3) IT INCLUDES THE MINISTRY OF DELIVERANCE

Casting out devils and restoring those who have been delivered to perfect soundness of mind and body, lies beyond the scope of simple healing. An act of divine power is needed to drive out a demon and to re-create wholeness in a formerly tormented life; and the same may apply to people who are slaves to drug addiction.

Those suggestions are confirmed by the manner in which healing the sick and casting out demons are several times linked together - see Mt 10:1-2; Mk 16:17-18; Lu 9:1-2: 10:9, 17; Ac 8:6-7; etc. In Paul's mind, *"working miracles"*, when linked with gifts of healing, may have been synonymous with "casting out demons".

(4) IT IS LINKED WITH HOLY SPIRIT BAPTISM

The *"working of miracles"* may describe a special ministry of prayer and laying on of hands to impart the gift of the Holy Spirit. Simon sensed that a special authority was required for this ministry: *"Give me this power too, so that anyone upon whom I lay my hands may receive the Holy Spirit"* (Ac 8:19). But Peter angrily rebuked him, saying that such a ministry was the *"gift"* of God (vs. 20).

Perhaps that explains why the evangelist Philip failed to pray for his Samaritan converts himself. He may have felt that imparting Holy Spirit baptism to large numbers of people lay beyond the scope of his calling; so he was content to ask the apostles to come down from Jerusalem to *"pray for them to receive the Holy Spirit"* (vs. 14-15). Jesus' statement that the church can perform *"greater works"* (Jn 14:12) than he did may include this immense privilege of giving the Holy Spirit to believers through prayer and the laying on of hands.

(5) SPECIAL MIRACLES

"Working miracles" may include such *"signs and wonders"* as a supernatural haul of fish (Lu 5:4-8; Jn 21:4-8); turning water into wine (Jn 2:7-10); withering a fig tree (Mt 21:18-22; and notice how Christ specifically said that such miracles are possible to us); raising the dead (Ac 9:36-41); acts of judgment (Ac 5:1-12; 13:6-11); and compare also the many special miracles wrought by several (but not all) of the prophets of Israel.

III. THE GIFTS OF UTTERANCE

(A) PROPHECY

"Prophecy" involves both *forth*-telling and *fore*-telling, but in neither case is it a product of human ingenuity - if it were, it would be false

(cp. Je 23:16-22, etc). It is not ordinary preaching (although true "pentecostal" preaching may often rise to the level of anointed prophesying). It is instead a message to the church spoken by sudden inspiration (although a "prophet" can assist that inspiration by creating an environment into which divine revelation can flow - 2 Kg 3:15; Ro 12:6).

"Prophecy", then, is a message, revelation, exhortation, or prediction given by God, and spoken under the anointing of the Holy Spirit, un-premeditated, unprepared. It is an activity of the human spirit, moved upon by the Holy Spirit, and not a function of the human mind.

Later in this book I will give a more detailed exposition of the gift of prophecy, and also of the two other gifts of utterance; here it will be sufficient to note-

(1) We must distinguish between the ***gift of prophecy*** and the ***office of a prophet.*** The gift of prophecy seems to have been common in the early church; but, in the sense of a clearly defined and officially regarded class, there were only a limited number of prophets. Paul says that *"all may prophecy"* (1 Co 12:29), while a prophet is a special person given by Christ to the whole church. But whether expressed through a gifted prophet or an ordinary member of the congregation, prophecy remains a *gift* set in the local assembly by the Holy Spirit.

(2) There were certain *"prophets"* in the early church accord-ing to Ac 13:1 and Ep 4:11, and there are even more specific references in Ac 11:27-28 and 21:10 (note the contrast here with vs. 9, showing the difference between Philip's daughters, who *prophesied*, and Agabus, who was a *prophet*). Such prophets did not necessarily always express their ministry in the *gift* of prophecy; but they did always convey Spirit-given revelation, possibly by means of the gift of the word of knowledge.

(3) When a prophetic revelation was given in the early church, it contained no binding instruction. It never controlled either the decisions or the actions of the person(s) addressed. In Israel the prophets gave both *revelation* and *command;* but in the church a prophet may only *reveal*; he or she cannot *direct* the saints. Why? Because every believer is a member of the body of Christ, and a "priest" before God. In Christ we possess the highest possible dignity and status. No prophet has authority to take away from any believer his or her freedom in Christ, nor to strip from us our right to decide for ourselves what is or is not a divine instruction (cp. 1 Co 14:29). Notice, for example, how the prophet Agabus foretold a famine (Ac 21:11); but any action taken in the light of his oracle was the sole responsibility of the persons concerned. See Ac 11:29; 21:4, 10-14. Silas too was a prophet and Paul's companion, but Paul did not look to him for guidance (Ac 16:9-10).

(4) The gift of prophecy is seldom useful for foretelling the future, and in cases where predictions of the future are given they must be subject to the acid test - do they come to pass? If they do not, then that "prophecy" was not from the Holy Spirit, but from either one of two sources - the human mind, or demonic power. The latter would no doubt be rare and (to spiritual minds) obvious cases. As a general rule, if a prophecy (or interpretation of tongues) is not inspired by the Holy Spirit then it comes from the natural mind. Since any prophecy may be subject to natural influence, no oracle should be regarded as infallible; every prophetic word must remain subject to judgment by the hearer(s) (1 Co 14:29; 1 Th 5:19-22).

(5) The purpose of the gift of prophecy, according to Paul, is fivefold: *"upbuilding, encouragement, consolation, edification, learning"* (1 Co 14:3, 4-5,12,31). The important rule to follow in ascertaining the value and orderliness of this gift is simply whether or not it fulfils this divine purpose. If it does, it is good; if not, it should be rejected.

(B) THE GIFT OF TONGUES

What are these tongues? The relevant historical passages (Ac 2:1-11; 10:44-48; 19:1-6) show that they are a powerful, usually fervent utterance, in a language that is unknown to the speaker. It is a miraculous work of the Holy Spirit enabling people to speak in a language of which they have no natural knowledge. As such, it is a supernatural gift.[a]

The scriptures show three areas of Christian experience in which glossolalia may occur -

(1) AS A SIGN OF HOLY SPIRIT BAPTISM

This use of glossolalia is dealt with fully in the companion book to this volume, *Clothed With Power*; so I will not comment any further here on the evidential, or confirmatory, values of glossolalia.

(2) AS A MEANS OF PERSONAL EDIFICATION

See 1 Co 14:2,3,18. These references do not deal with glossolalia as the initial sign of Holy Spirit baptism, for they are addressed to people who had already experienced that baptism. They refer rather to the continuing exercise of glossolalic prayer in private devotions and in general worship. Paul describes this devotional use of glossolalia as a deep and inspired communion with God (1 Co 14:2), which he himself frequently enjoyed (vs. 18). To him it was a fine means of *"giving thanks"* (vs. 14-16).

---

[a] That is, Christian glossolalia, in its first occurrence in a person's life, arises from a supernatural impulse (that is, Holy Spirit baptism). But after that initial event, as my later comments will show, glossolalia becomes a natural function of the human spirit, and may or may not carry the anointing of the Holy Spirit.

(3) AS A SOURCE OF PROPHETIC ORACLES

See 1 Co 12:10,30; 14:5, 13,26-27. In this use, the glossolalist does not speak to God, but rather addresses the congregation, expecting that his or her utterance will be interpreted so that the church may be instructed and strengthened.

(C) THE INTERPRETATION OF TONGUES

This gift is indispensable for any prophetic use of glossolalia in the church.   Interpretation conveys to the *minds* of the hearers the message that has come from the *spirit* of the glossolalist.   But although the gift of interpretation is expressed in the vernacular of the congregation, it should still retain the quality of a supernatural utterance, parallel to prophecy in its nature and origin.

Chapter Three

MADE FOR MIRACLES

Having established that spiritual gifts really did exist in the early church, we can advance to a second area in which people are ignorant: *the true nature of the charismata.* And here I want to emphasise three things:-

I. THEY ARE SUPERNATURAL

There is a sense, of course, in which every gift or ability that God has given us, including natural endowments, may be described as a divine *"charis"* - see Paul's intermingled list of "natural" and "supernatural" giftings in *Romans 12:3-8.* However, it is certain that Paul did not have natural abilities in mind when he composed his list of various gifts in *1 Corinthians 12:8-10.* We cannot suppose that these essentially spiritual manifestations (*pneumatika*) consist of nothing more than natural ability inspired and enlarged by the Holy Spirit. Some have suggested, for example, that the gifts of healing are now fulfilled in Christian physicians and hospitals. Others claim that the gift of tongues, is now fulfilled through missionary linguistic schools, or in the translation of the scriptures into many dialects and languages. But Paul's description shows plainly enough that the charismata have little connection with natural accomplishments: they are divine endowments wrought in the believer by the Holy Spirit; they are supernatural both in origin and in character.

There are of course varying degrees of human agency mixed in with the manifestation of these gifts, which is why some of the charismata are more open than others to wrongful use.

Human agency appears least of all in the three gifts of inspiration: *the word of wisdom, the word of knowledge,* and *the discerning of spirits.* The purpose of those gifts is **revelation**. Their manifestation is more *to* the believer than *through* the believer. Since the occurrence of revelation gifts requires little or no overt action by the believer, Paul says little about their control or exercise, nor does he offer any correction concerning their use.

More of human agency appears in the gifts of *faith, healing* and *miracles*. These are gifts of **power**, they create a definite effect on people and things, they appeal to the senses. However, because these spiritual gifts occur in connection with a specific ministry function, which cannot be effective unless it is pervaded and controlled by the Holy Spirit, Paul once again gives no instruction for their use, nor any correction of their abuse. Misuse of these gifts cannot continue, because the introduction of wrong conduct will destroy the person's ministry and the charismata will be nullified.

Human agency appears most of all in *prophecy, tongues* and *interpretation*. These three gifts, since they are dependent upon the faculty of speech, require the use of someone's voice. For this reason, they can be subjected to much misuse, hence Paul devotes an entire chapter (1 Co 14) to instruction about their proper function.

This varying degree of human involvement in the exercise of the charismata is the reason for the disproportionate amount of space Paul gives to describing some of them while he virtually ignores others. In fact scripture provides no detailed explanation of any of the charismata except the gifts of utterance. The others are sufficiently defined in the relevant historical accounts in the *Gospels*, the *Acts*, and the *Letters*. If they occur, they occur correctly, because they cannot function in any other way. The gifts of utterance, by contrast, can be used as readily in a wrong setting as in a right one. Moreover, the frequent occurrence of the gifts of utterance in the worship of the church makes it more necessary to receive detailed instruction about their use.

Do not let the varied level of human involvement in the charismata diminish your appreciation of their supernatural character. Although some of them may be in some respects associated with human ability, true charismata will never be merely the product of natural skill. They must remain, at least in their fundamental origin and nature, *"manifestations of the Holy Spirit"*, supernaturally given to the church *"for the common good"* (12:7).

II. THEY ARE OVERLAPPING

Previously I divided the nine gifts of the Spirit into the following classifications:

> *The Gifts of Revelation*
> - wisdom, knowledge, discernment
> *The Gifts of Power*
> - faith, healing, miracles
> *The Gifts of Utterance*
> - prophecy, tongues, interpretation

That is a reasonable classification. Why then is it not set out like that in scripture? I suggest that by his apparently random listing of nine charismata, Paul is showing (perhaps unconsciously) that it is wrong to isolate these gifts from each other, or to think of them as functioning independently of each other. Look at the way Paul has composed his list:

- there are two *revelation* gifts, and one *power* gift:
  - wisdom, knowledge, faith

- then two *power* gifts, and one *utterance* gift
  - healing, miracles, prophecy

- finally one *revelation* gift, and two *utterance* gifts
  - discernment, tongues, interpretation

This lack of any obvious order suggests that the gifts were not clearly delineated in Paul's mind. It is almost as though on the spur of the moment he decided to list a few of the things that were evidence of the charismatic work of the Holy Spirit in the church. There is no more reason to suppose that this list is final or definitive than to suppose the same of his lists of spiritual "fruit" (cp. Ga 5:22-23; Ro 14:17; Cl 3:12-15; etc). All those lists appear to be arbitrary, with no formal structure. They are simply indicative of the kind of things the Holy Spirit may be expected to accomplish in believers and in the church.

However, it remains convenient for us to read a more or less formal structure into Paul's lists. We do so for the sake of comparison and explanation; and there is no harm in this, so long as it is remembered that Paul himself had no such rigid pattern in mind.

So I am suggesting that it is improper to draw a sharp dividing line between the gifts of the Spirit - they will normally occur in fusion with other gifts and in conjunction with the general ministry operating in the church. It is true, of course, that at times one gift may be more prominent than the others; but seldom (with the possible exception of the gifts of utterance) will a gift be exercised in complete isolation from any other manifestation of the Spirit. Even the gifts of utterance will frequently be intermingled with, or contain, other gifts of revelation; and faith, as a gift, will often be an essential prerequisite for the highest exercise of any gift -

"The story of Paul's sea voyage as a prisoner on the ill-fated ship reveals the overlapping of at least five of the spiritual manifestations. First, THE WORD OF KNOWLEDGE was given him as to the course to pursue to save the lives of those on board. Second, FAITH, for he said, `Sirs, I believe God'. It required supernatural faith for an occasion of that nature, when not only their ship was in danger, but their lives likewise. Third, THE WORD OF WISDOM was given to him. The shipmen were lowering the boats to escape to shore. The soldiers had in mind to kill the prisoners lest they escape. Had this disorderly abandonment of the ship been permitted, the soldiers would have carried out their purpose to kill the prisoners, including Paul. Paul, with the word of wisdom from God, spoke to the centurion and said, 'Unless these abide on the ship, we cannot be saved.' The ropes were immediately cut and the boats fell into the water. This word of wisdom saved Paul's life, as well as the lives of the other prisoners.

"Then there came a command from the centurion to abandon ship. It was carried out in an orderly way and they all MIRACULOUSLY reached land safely, so that there was no necessity to kill the prisoners. Later, as Paul put a bundle of sticks on the fire, a viper, a venomous beast, fastened itself on his hand. A MIRACLE saved Paul's life for he shook it off and it did him no harm. Then Paul entered into a house on the island and healed a man of fever and a bloody flux. Following this, many people on the island who were ill came and WERE HEALED. We have here five of the manifestations of the Spirit in operation; namely, THE WORD OF KNOWLEDGE, FAITH, THE WORD OF WISDOM, MIRACLES, and HEALING. Paul SPOKE IN TONGUES, PROPHESIED, INTERPRETED and had DISCERNMENT; thus, it is apparent that all the manifestations were evident in his life."

This overlapping of the gifts is seen also in the healing of the lame man at the "Beautiful" gate of the Temple:

"This man was carried there daily. Peter and John were in the habit of going to the temple to pray. They undoubtedly contacted him on other occasions. This morning it was different. Peter got THE WORD OF KNOWLEDGE that it was the will of God to heal him. He was not only HEALED INSTANTLY, but HIS FEET AND ANKLE BONES RECEIVED STRENGTH so that he went into the Temple WALKING, LEAPING AND PRAISING GOD. In Acts 3:16, Peter explained it was FAITH IN JESUS' NAME that made this man whole. We see, therefore, that at least four of the manifestations of 1 Cor 12 were employed in the healing of this cripple. First, THE WORD OF KNOWLEDGE; second, HEALING; third, MIRACLE;

fourth, FAITH; and it is reasonably probable that there was DISCERNMENT." [a]

You might want to quarrel with some of the applications made by that author, and perhaps I would too; but I think he has well expressed the proper manner in which the charismata (excluding the gifts of utterance) occurred in the early church. There was a more or less unconscious, yet continuous occurrence of "signs, wonders, and various gifts of the Holy Spirit" (He 2:4) confirming all their ministry. I say "unconscious" because the gifts so intermingled with each other and with the circumstances that the people involved may often not have been aware that a spiritual gift was at work. Perhaps only as they looked back did they perceive that God had met their need through one or more of the charismata. On other occasions, of course, say when a visible miracle took place, there could be no doubt that a spiritual gift had been demonstrated.

A further example of this overlapping and interweaving of the gifts is seen in 1 Co 14:6 where Paul describes a message in tongues, followed by an interpretation that included (or could include) "revelation" (the word of wisdom), "knowledge" (the word of knowledge) "prophesying", "doctrine" (cp. verse 3 "edification, exhortation, comfort").

This lack of clear definition in many of the charismata is confirmed by the imprecise terminology used by Paul. For example, no article occurs in his list of the gifts. He writes, *"To one is given utterance of wisdom, to another utterance of knowledge ... etc."* In this way he draws attention to the general nature of the gifts rather than to their individuality.

---

[a] Many years ago I copied those passages from a book that I have long since loaned and lost. I have forgotten the title of the book, and the author's name I have recorded only as 'McAlister'.

Likewise, he uses random terminology when he describes the manner in which the charismata are bestowed -

"through the Spirit" (vs. 8*)*
"according to the same Spirit" (vs. 8)
"by the same Spirit" (vs. 9)
"by the one Spirit" (vs. 9)
"inspired by one and the same Spirit" (vs. 11)

Once again the impression given (apart from a desire for literary variety) is that Paul was trying to avoid any kind of stereotyped pattern for the gifts, both in their nature and in the manner in which they operate. He simply describes those things that are generally characteristic of the Spirit's working in the church. In fact, Paul himself elsewhere gave different lists of charismata: Ro 12:6-8; 1 Co 12:28,29-30; 13:1-2,8; Ep 4:11. In each of those lists he adds to, subtracts from, and uses a random order for the gifts (a fact, by the way, that nullifies the contention that "glossolalia" - because it is placed last in 1 Co 12:10 - is therefore the "least" gift). There are also other passages that list manifestations of the Spirit apart from those cited by Paul:

– Ac 2:2-3, 17-18, 4:31; He 2:4 (where we read about *"gifts of the Holy Spirit"*, <u>plus</u> *"signs, wonders, and miracles"*.

Someone may argue that the different descriptions can all be fitted into the categories cited by Paul in 1 Co 12:8-10. I reply that to do so broadens the categories so much that the same effect is achieved; namely, such a diffusion of the boundaries of the charismata leads to an inescapable loss of clear definition.

So, although Paul has recorded nine spiritual gifts, we make a mistake if we try to parcel them neatly and limit them to the precise names and number stated by the apostle. Those who understand this will resist any tendency toward claiming permanent possession of a particular gift, with its resulting exaltation of a person. Perhaps nowhere in the New Testament is there a sharply defined account of an exercise of one isolated gift. But we do find everywhere a record of the moving of the Holy Spirit, which resulted generally in healings, exorcisms, revelations, and many other signs, wonders and spiritual manifestations.

Therefore Paul's list is general rather than specific; it is indicative, not definitive. It portrays the kind of manifestations that characterise the ministry of the Holy Spirit in the church. And, save the possible exception of the voice gifts, those various manifestations of the Spirit normally occur together, mingled and overlapping.

III. THEY ARE INDISPENSABLE

Paul said that God has "set" various charismatic gifts and ministries in the church (1 Co 12:28). The Greek word is *"tithemi,* [a]and it is in the middle voice, which means that it carries the sense: *"for his own special purpose God has placed (sundry functions) in the church."* To ignore any of those gifts or ministries is to thwart that divine purpose. What are they? Paul lists eight items, all of which he says God has "set" (*tithemi*) in the church:

– apostles
– prophets
– teachers
– miracle-workers
– gifts of healing
– skilled helpers
– administrators
– gift of tongues.

Notice how carelessly Paul intertwines the natural and the supernatural, the earthly and the heavenly, the human and the divine. Such a casual mixture suggests that Paul refused to make any sharp

---

[a] This word is discussed more fully in Chapter Five

distinctions between the various items;[a] he declined to say that one was intrinsically "better" than another. They are all vital to the good health of the church. Nonetheless, it is useful for us to break the eight functions into two groups: *natural*, and *supernatural* -

(A) NATURAL

There are four functions whose success depends mainly upon careful planning and hard work: *"apostles, teachers, helpers, administrators."* Of course, no amount of human skill or effort can compensate for a lack of the grace, wisdom, and power of the Holy Spirit. Nonetheless, these functions may be seen primarily as *natural* talents enhanced by the Spirit, rather than as *supernatural* gifts enhanced by human effort.

(B) SUPERNATURAL

There are four functions whose success depends mainly upon supernatural revelation and divine action: *"prophets, healers, miracle-workers, glossolalists."* The sad thing is that just as I have separated the eight functions above, so they are often separated in church life. In other words, there are churches that can be described wholly in terms of the first group of natural functions; and others that can be described wholly in terms of the second group of supernatural functions.

Look at some churches and say, *"apostles, teachers, helpers, administrators,"* and you have said all that can be said about them. Look at others and say, *"prophets, healers, miracle-workers, glossolalists,"* and again you have said all that is worth saying. Neither description is healthy. Why? Because those who embrace only natural functions, and reject the supernatural, are always prone to

---

[a] This idea is discussed more fully in the next Chapter

lapse into an arid intellectualism; while those who follow the reverse practice seldom avoid the trap of shallow emotionalism.

We ought to shun both snares, and determine to pattern our churches according to scripture, and to allow the Holy Spirit to produce in them the full range of gifts and ministries appointed by God. Paul unconsciously enforced that principle when he avoided the mistake (which I have committed above) of separating the eight functions from each other. He mingled them easily - the natural with the supernatural, the miraculous with the mundane - because he knew that unless they all flourished together the church would fail in its mission.

Chapter Four

STILL AVAILABLE

In the church at Corinth there were apparently some people who wanted to abolish all spiritual gifts, and there were others who felt that only a privileged few could enjoy the charismata. The same misinformation is rife today. In this chapter we look at three common errors and an answer to them-

(A) "CHARISMATA ENDED WITH THE APOSTLES"

In 1 Co 13:8-10 Paul declares that spiritual gifts will one day pass away. This passage is often used by our opponents to prove that the charismata, having fulfilled their purpose, ended when the New Testament was completed and the early church was firmly established. But when will *"prophecies pass away"*? When will *"tongues cease"*? When will *"knowledge pass away"*? Paul answers, *"when the perfect comes, the imperfect will pass away."*

What is "the perfect"? Is it really the completed canon of scripture, or the perfected church? The first of those questions hardly deserves to be taken seriously. The second is close to the truth. The "perfection" referred to by Paul is certainly the perfected church - but it is equally certainly not the early church as such. Commentators of every persuasion (when they are not grinding an axe against Pentecostals) are happily agreed that Paul is talking about the perfection the church will obtain when it is finally glorified in heaven. Until then, at least outwardly, the church will remain incomplete, imperfect, with new members ("babes in Christ") being added continually. So we could paraphrase Paul (vs. 12) -

> *"For now (in this present time) we see in a mirror*
> *dimly (our knowledge and experience are alike*
> *incomplete); but* then *(when Christ comes) we shall*
> *see face to face. Now I (Paul) know in part (despite*
> *great revelation and many spiritual gifts); then (and*
> *only then) I shall understand fully, even as I have*
> *been fully understood."*

There is simply no way in which Paul's references to "then" and "face to face" can be reasonably understood as pointing to the completed canon of scripture. Paul knew more gospel truth (2 Co 12:1-4) than any other person has ever known, and he probably had a richer experience of the charismata (Ro 15:18-19; 1 Co 15:10); but he still reckoned that he had not yet reached spiritual manhood. He still yearned for the great day when he would stand *"face to face"* with Christ; for then, and only then, would he truly be perfected.

Paul illustrates this fact of our present imperfection, hence of our continuing need for the charismata, by the example of ordinary human growth -

> *"When I was a child, I spoke like a child, I thought*
> *like a child, I reasoned like a child; but when I*
> *became a man I gave up childish ways" (vs. 11).*

The lesson is simple. During the time of growth to maturity children need many things to augment their partial understanding and to assist them in their development into adulthood. But when they reach full maturity they gladly put away the toys and tools of children. It is tragic for a grown man to retain the ways of infancy, pitied as an imbecile. And it is equally sad to see a child thinking itself already an adult. Arrogant precocity is disliked by all:

- "A man at sixteen will prove a child at sixty".
  (Thomas Fuller)
- "Precocious youth is a sign of premature death".
  (Pliny)

–   "He who is wise before his time will die before he is old".
    (Latin Proverb)

Just as it is unnatural for a child to despise the things that belong to childhood, so Christians should not scorn the things that belong to our present state. That state is one of spiritual "childhood". We speak as children (that is, in other tongues, in prophecy, etc.); we understand as children (that is, we need to be taught in a way that indicates our immaturity); we reason, and think, and behave, as children, not yet having reached full adulthood in Christ. When we do reach that maturity (in the resurrection) we will put away all "childish" things; until then we need them.

So at present we are still growing and developing (Ep 4:11-13). Our ultimate goal is perfection in Christ; but we reach that perfection by means of things that are, by comparison, imperfect. Naturally, when the end is reached, the means will be abolished; then tongues, and prophecies, and all the fragmentary gifts of the Spirit will cease.

When will that end be reached?

When we see our Lord "face to face".

And the means God has provided to bring us to that end are the gifts of the Spirit and the ministry gifts of Christ. These are the things of our "childhood". Yet it must sadden the Lord to see so many of his children precociously thinking themselves to be "adults" already, and spurning the precious gifts he has provided to bring us to maturity. In ordinary life, if children refuse the toys, blocks, and tools of childhood their growth will be warped and stunted. The same thing happens when the church rejects the diverse gifts of the Spirit. So let us desire these gifts, and make use of them, for they help us to "grow up" in Christ. At the same time, remain aware of their relative value, humbly recognising that their very use shows our littleness before the Lord.

That the gifts of the Spirit are adapted only to this present state of growth into maturity is clear from their very nature. Even in their best operation the charismata are narrow in compass and temporary in revelation. It is today as it was of old. Even the great prophets and inspired apostles had only a slight knowledge of the infinite wonders of God and of his eternal glory. Truly the most capable of people only *"know in part and prophecy in part"*. Love alone is the one thing we can fully encompass in this life that will abide eternally.

So it is with little children. The infant endowments they receive are essential to their growth, yet quickly pass away. But love remains, only deepening and broadening with the passage of years.

When we see God face to face, and know him as we are now known, all else will fall away from us except *faith, hope, love* - and even of those *love* is reckoned the greatest (1 Co 13:13)

Matthew Henry writes -

"*Faith* fixes on the divine revelation and assents to that; hope fastens on future felicity, and waits for that; and in heaven faith will be swallowed up in vision, and hope in fruition. There is no room to believe and hope when we see and enjoy".

But in that perfection to come, *love* will find only greater objects for its passion, greater delight in its praise. There, all shackles of space and time will be cast off, and love will burst forth in glorious splendour, the source of endless rivers of pleasure to both lover and loved alike!

Clearly then we may affirm that:

- ◆ spiritual gifts (as in 1 Co 12:8-10) and even ministry gifts (as in Ep 4:11) are adapted to a state of imperfection, of "childhood";
- ◆ such things are yet entirely essential to our present state, for they are the means by which we shall reach perfection.
- ◆ that state once reached, the things of "childhood" will pass away, no further use being found for them.

- we should therefore desire spiritual gifts, but only with a view to eternity and the perfection that is to come, always *"following after love"*, which alone abides always (1 Co 14:1).

(B) "CHARISMATA BELONG TO THE CHOSEN FEW"

That the gifts of the Spirit are in fact available to every member of the church may be learned from the way Paul describes their distribution and operation. He uses six different words (including a reference from the anonymous *Letter to the Hebrews):*

- *"charisma"*1 Co 12:4,9,31; etc. = a gift of grace, a spiritual endowment
- *"pneumatikos"* - 1 Co 12:1; 14:1,12; etc. = a spiritual manifestation
- *"phanerosis"* - 1 Co 12:7 = a manifestation
- *"diairesis"* - 1 Co 12:4,5,6,11 (*diaireo*) = to divide into parts, to distribute
- *"energeo"* - 1 Co 12:11 = to work in, or through
- *"merismos"* - He 2:4 = a dividing, a distribution.

Collected together, those words give a good picture of the true nature of the charismata:

- *"energeo"* emphasises that they are a result of the inner, and supernatural working of the Holy Spirit
- *"charisma"* confirms their character as free gifts, arising from the rich grace of God, always beyond the reach of human earning capacity
- *"pneumatikos"* and *"phanerosis"* stress that the charismata are in fact simply a brief and striking manifestation of the indwelling Spirit himself
- *"diairesis"* and *"merismos"* show that the charismata are all fragments of the Spirit's power and ability, divided freely to "each" member of the church in order to serve "the common good" (1 Co 12:7.11).

Clearly then, while we may speak of spiritual *"gifts"* we must qualify that thought by the expression spiritual *"manifestations"*. The charismata are not "gifts" in the ordinary sense of something given to become someone's personal property. They are "gifts" because they are imparted gratuitously, as unmerited favours of God. However, they do not become the private possession of the recipient, to be exercised at will. [a]

The charismata are not gifts given *by* the Holy Spirit *to* believers, so much as manifestations of the Holy Spirit *through* believers. Hence they are spoken of as *"the working"* of the Holy Spirit himself, who distributes these gifts freely *"to each person individually as he pleases"* (1 Co 12:11). Nowhere in scripture is there a clear statement that one or another spiritual gift will be given permanently to any person. Rather, biblical emphasis falls upon the Holy Spirit manifesting himself by means of various charismata through the whole church - first through this member, then that member, and so on.

In other words, every Spirit-filled believer has a potential capacity for every gift of the Spirit; they are not the purview of a privileged few.

That idea is confirmed by Paul's careful statement, *"there are varieties of gifts, but the same Spirit"* (vs. 7). [b] His emphasis does not fall upon possession of the gifts but upon possession of the Holy Spirit, who is the source of all the gifts. The Corinthians were apparently singling out certain charismata for special honour. They

---

[a] Glossolalia, for reasons that are explained below, is an exception to this rule. Unlike the other charismata, glossolalia become permanent once it has been imparted to someone.

[b] Compare also "same spirit" (vs. 8); "same Spirit" (vs. 9); "the one Spirit (vs. 9); "one and the same Spirit(vs. 11); "by one Spirit (vs. 13); "of one Spirit" (vs. 13)

believed that these "higher" gifts showed a greater degree of spirituality, and that they elevated their users above others who exercised the "lesser" gifts. Paul insists rather that since all the gifts arise from the one great Gift - the Holy Spirit himself - it is absurd to set the various charismata against one another. So we are forbidden to value people by the spiritual gifts that happen to operate through them.

Further proof of the distinction between the "gift" (singular) of the Holy Spirit and the "gifts" (plural) of the Holy Spirit is seen in the two Greek words scripture uses to describe this difference. When talking about the "gift" of the Holy Spirit, the apostle used the word *"dorea"* = a gift given from an outside source, to become a permanent possession. The stress here is on the fact that the gift is *free* and *permanent* Ac 2:38; 8:20; 10:45; 11:17. But when it talks about the "gifts" of the Spirit, scripture uses the word *"charisma"* = a gift that is an act of kindness or favour. The stress here falls on the idea that the gift is an expression of divine *grace*, but it does not necessarily involve permanence - Ro 12:6; 1 Co 1:7; 12:4,9,28,30,31; 1 Pe 4:10. Note also that *"dorea"* is used in connection with the *"ministry gifts"* listed by Paul in Ep 4:7, intimating the permanence inherent in a call to service. A "ministry gift" - of pastor, evangelist, teacher, etc - is a "dorea", a permanent gift; but the charismata are variously occurring endowments, graciously imparted by the Holy Spirit to equip believers to fulfil the call of God. They are therefore normally manifested only in the course of fulfilling that call. If the "dorea" is changed by God, or for some reason withdrawn, then the "charismata" will also be changed or withdrawn.

Placing emphasis on the charismata as "manifestations" of the Spirit, rather than viewing them as settled gifts, helps to prevent any tendency to isolate each gift in a separate compartment bearing a special label - an attitude that has the ultimate effect of stifling the initiative of the Holy Spirit and of closing the Christian's life to a free flow of *"pneumatika"*.

As resident in the Holy Spirit, and being freely bestowed by him as he wills, these manifestations are called "gifts"; but in operation through a member of the body of Christ, these gifts are called "manifestations"!

A proper scriptural emphasis will also discourage people from claiming to have "this gift" or "that gift", which tends to inflate human ego and foolishly to set one spiritual gift against another. If we boast at all, or claim any gift at all, that gift must be the one that all Spirit-filled believers share in common: "the Gift (*dorea*) of the Holy Spirit" himself. The scriptures do not say that any person may possess any of the charismata as a permanent gift. But there is abundant evidence that all the charismata were manifested in various places, at various times, through various people, throughout the whole early church. Is there any real reason why we cannot see in this a happy paradigm for the church today?

(C) "CHARISMATA ARE FOR SPECIAL OCCASIONS"

I have shown that the charismata are available to every believer. But when? What does Paul mean, *"The Spirit distributes the gifts at will to each person individually"*? (12:11) Must we infer that each gift will occur only at the arbitrary and random choice of the Spirit? When does the Holy Spirit "will" to grant us his gifts?

The key is found in Paul's earlier comment: *"To each person the manifestation of the Spirit is given for the good of all"* (vs. 7). That is not just a statement of fact, it is also a promise. Will it be to the profit of the believer and the church for a particular gift to be manifested? Then you may be confident that the Spirit is willing to bestow that gift. Hence the apostle's words, *"earnestly desire the best gifts"* (1 Co 12:31). "Best" is *"meizon"* = greater, not in quality or nature, but more useful, or valuable. Hence, you should *"earnestly desire"* whatever gift is best for you or for the church at any particular time or place. No gift is in itself better than another; each has its own area of importance, its own useful function. Therefore, today this gift will be best, but tomorrow another, and the day after another again. On each occasion we should earnestly desire the gift that is "best" for that occasion.

The one qualification is that our desire for a certain gift, and our exercise of it, must be motivated by *"love"* (see 1 Co 13) - *"keep <u>love</u> as your aim, (and then) earnestly desire the gifts of the Spirit"* (14:1).

Chapter Five

HIGHLY PROFITABLE!

People really are uninformed on this issue! Many sincere Christians allow that the charismata are available today, yet still fail either to "desire" them "earnestly" or to experience them in their own worship and witness. They feel that spiritual gifts have little real value, and that the church can serve God just as effectively without them. Such claims would have stunned Paul, for he made two statements about the superb value of the charismata. In the first, he said that the charismata are "set" in the church; and in the second, that they are *"profitable"* for the church.

(A) THE CHARISMATA ARE 'SET' IN THE CHURCH

Twice Paul uses the Greek word *"tithemi"* in connection with the charismata (1 Co 12:18,28). *"tithemi"* means "to set in place, to appoint, to ordain, to establish". Those meanings show that the charismata have been planted in the church by the will of God, to function permanently as an integral part of its worship and witness. Paul confirms that by using *"tithemi"* in two particular ways, both of which highlight the ideas of permanency and continuity -

(1) "TITHEMI", AS A TECHNICAL RELIGIOUS EXPRESSION

> *"God has set (tithemi) in the church apostles, prophets, ... etc" (1 Co 12:28)*

Go back in imagination to the ancient city of Corinth, on a holy day in 50 A.D. A magnificent new temple has just been consecrated, but the idol for which it was built has not yet been installed. Now the day has come for the sacred image to be put in place upon the empty pedestal. All work in the city has stopped, and the streets are thronged with a merry crowd waiting for the colourful procession to pass by. The statue of the god finally comes into sight, carried by its priests, and accompanied by prayers, songs, burning incense, cascades of flower petals, musicians and dancing girls. The people shout and cheer, acclaiming their god, until the parade ends at the doors of the new temple. Then a hush falls over the crowd as with great dignity the priests carry the idol into the sacred place and reverently install it in the inmost sanctuary. Word is carried out to the people that the god has now taken up residence in his new house, and mighty are their shouts of joy!

The technical religious term used by the Greeks to describe the act of formally installing a god or goddess in a temple was *"tithemi"*. Indeed, until the *"tithemi"* had taken place, the temple remained simply a building, with no sacred significance. But the arrival of the idol at once turned it into a holy temple. Now sacrifices can be offered there, and worship can be presented. Even the precincts of the building must be treated reverently, and profane actions will be severely punished. Nothing less than the presence of the god could turn a pile of masonry into a divine place, a hallowed place of prayer and praise.

But suppose after many years the sacred image were to be removed, what then? The temple would become again merely another building, an empty shell, lacking divine purpose or power. Its sanctity, its religious significance, its value to the community, all depended upon the idol being *"set"* in its proper place.

Against that background, notice how Paul contrasts the *"dumb"* idols that were "set" in the heathen temples, with the living manifestations of the Spirit that are "set" in the church (vs. 2). He is showing two things -

    (a) Despite the *"tithemi"*, the temples of the heathen still remained hollow husks, for their deities were *"dumb"* - unable to hear the cry of a petitioner, unable to speak a word of answer, unable to work a miracle. Their worship was a delusion, their service a pathway to despair.

(b) By contrast, the living God has performed a true *"tithemi"* by setting in his church the gifts of the Holy Spirit, which do speak and act with power. Through them the presence of the Lord is revealed, by them the prayers of the people are answered.

But we may add another conclusion: just as surely as the purpose of a heathen temple was void if the *"tithemi"* did not occur, so the church is made less effective[a] if it does not allow the Holy Spirit to *"set in place"* (tithemi) the charismata.

It follows then that these gifts are beneficial to the worship of the people; remove them from the house of God and Christian liturgy may become as empty of divine response as was the idolatrous worship of old.

The church was created specifically to house the charismata; it exists to provide a setting in which the charismata can flourish. What then should be said of those people who refuse to allow the appointment in their worship of the very things for which the church was built? Such folly creates an anomaly nearly as great (say) as if the pagan Ephesians had built their splendid temple for Diana and had then refused to allow the goddess to be set up there!

Worship in which nothing can be observed except the voice and works of the people is only half-worship. Full Christian worship requires the presence of voice and works of God. How can that be

---

[a] Why do I say "less" effective rather than ineffective"? Because wherever there is genuine Faith in God there must be at least some working of the Holy Spirit, some expression of his presence and power, even if those people know nothing about the Holy Spirit baptism or about the charismata

achieved? Only by the charismata, which God has already set in the church. But they cannot function without human cooperation, through prayer, faith, and active use (cp. 1 Co 12:31a, *"earnestly desire the charismata"*; 14:12, *"you are eager for the gifts of the Spirit"*; Ro 12:6a, *"let us use the various gifts God has given to us."*)

(2) "TITHEMI", IN RELATION TO THE HUMAN BODY

Paul uses *"tithemi"* in a second sense, related to the structure of the human body (1 Co 12:18) -

> *"God has set (tithemi) each member of your body in*
> *its appointed place, according to his own pleasure."*

When we read that God is the one who *"set"* our *"members"* in our bodies, we understand at once what the apostle means: God himself designed the human body with all its parts, and declared that every part should have its necessary and valuable function. Nor do the members of our bodies despise one another, or say that they have no need of each other (vs. 14-21). We are in fact very reluctant to part with even the least member of our bodies. Every piece of the body that is removed causes a loss to the whole body (vs. 26).

So, too, with the church, the "body" of Christ (vs. 27). After all, the members of our physical bodies are not garments or ornaments that we can put on or take off at will; they are integral parts of the body, and are essential to its wellbeing and proper functioning. When Paul follows *verse 18* (which deals with the body) with *verse 28* (which deals with the charismata), we cannot doubt that he saw them as analogous to each other. That is, the charismata hold the same relationship to the church as our limbs do our bodies. Are you willing to dispense with several parts of your body? Hardly! Then neither should you be willing for the church to be denied the charismata.

Has the human body changed in its parts and functions over the centuries? No! Is it still fitting to describe the church as having a structure analogous to that of the human body? Yes! Then the apostle's argument must remain in force: the charismata are an irreplaceable part of the church. A church from which the charismata have been excised may remain alive, still functioning as the body of Christ; but it will inevitably be sadly crippled. Such a disabled church must fall short of God's ideal, just as the human body would if several limbs or organs were removed from it. How healthy, how effective, is a limbless man, lacking arms, legs, ears, and eyes. He may still be alive, but he is not much use, either to himself or anyone else!

Some have argued that the charismata were given to the church only during its formative years, but after the death of the apostles they were withdrawn by God. But Paul's analogy of the human body precludes this. Has God's design and purpose for the human body changed? Do we need our limbs any less now than people did twenty centuries ago? Again the answer must be, "No!" Then neither has the church changed, nor does it have any less need of the charismata.

As it happens, the pattern of the human body will not change until the day of Christ's return and of the resurrection of the dead; only then will we discard our physical organs and assume a new form (Ph 3:31; 1 Co 15:51-53; 2 Co 5:1-5). And that is exactly when the church will be able to discard the charismata (1 Co 13:8-12). But for now, just as surely as I still need my hands, feet, eyes, ears, so the church still needs the charismata. I could no more think of rejecting them than I could of dismembering my own body.

(B) THE CHARISMATA ARE "PROFITABLE"

Paul declared, *"To each person the manifestation of the Spirit is given for the common good"* (1 Co 12:7). *"Common good"* translates a phrase that is based upon the Greek word *"sumphero"* = "profitable, advantageous, beneficial".

Elsewhere in the New Testament *"sumphero"* is used in connection with -

♦ the profit the whole world gained from the death of Christ (Jn 11:50; 18:14); and with

- ♦ the profit the church has gained from the ascension of Christ (Jn 16:7); and with
- ♦ the profit we gain from imputed holiness (He 12:10).

Those verses provide a good sense of the breadth of meaning that lies in *"sumphero"*. And insofar as the charismata are inextricably liked with the death, resurrection, and ascension of Christ, and with the practical outworking of holiness, it is a fair inference to say that they convey on the *pragmatic* level the same "profitability" that those other matters convey on the *forensic* level. That is, what has been legally and potentially made available to us in the heavenlies in Christ can be brought into earthly reality through the charismata.

But whether or not that inference is accepted, it cannot be denied that scripture affirms the genuine profitability of the charismata in the church. They work *"for the common good"*: their influence is beneficial; they heighten the ministry of the Spirit in the church. For my part, I find it difficult to follow the logic of those who feel that they may easily dispense with things that God says are designed to profit them. Are we so rich that we can afford to reject even the least of God's favours?

Chapter Six

LOVE IS BEST

Three things must be said about the proper use of the charismata -

(I) THEY MUST BE EXERCISED IN LOVE

(A) CHARISMATA AND CHARACTER

Paul wrote, "Earnestly desire the higher gifts; yet I will show you <u>a still more excellent way</u>" (1 Co 12:31).

What is this "*more excellent way*"? The following verses (13:1-13) show that it is to *"follow after love"*. Now there are two possible ways to understand this passage -

(1) PAUL WAS REBUKING THE CORINTHIANS

Some prefer to read Paul's instruction like this: *"You are greatly envious for what you reckon are the highest gifts; but I want to show you a far better way"* That reading is supported by verse four of the next chapter, where the same Greek word is used: *"love is not jealous."*

If that is what Paul meant, then he was rebuking the Corinthians for envy, not telling them to pray. They should have humbly recognised their proper place in the body of Christ, and then trusted God to bestow the charismata as he saw fit. Instead, they were quarrelling with each other, striving for precedence, and were wrongly jealous of each other's gifts and callings.

The gifts of the Spirit are infinitely valuable; but if they become a source of pride and confusion then they will bring only loss to those who exercise them.

Therefore Paul exhorted the Corinthians to walk in love toward each other and God. Then the Spirit of God would be able to manifest in them freely a glorious diversity of gifts, which would bring honour to their church and praise to the Lord.

However, the verse is more commonly taken to mean that

(2) PAUL WAS ENCOURAGING THE CORINTHIANS

In view of the first words of chapter fourteen this seems to be the more likely explanation. Compare these two verses -

> *"Earnestly desire the higher gifts; yet I will show you a still more excellent way" (12:31).*

> *"Make love your aim, and earnestly desire the spiritual gifts" (14:1).*

While the order is reversed, it is clear that both verses contain the same two instructions:

(a) we should desire and pray for the gifts of the Spirit

(b) but we must be very sure always to walk in the way of love.

What is this *"love"*?

Does he mean that while people of lower spirituality may crave spiritual gifts, those who are more mature prefer to display love? Hardly. The theme of the thirteenth chapter, set between chapters twelve and fourteen, is not a damaging comparison between love and spiritual gifts, with the latter being routed by the former. Rather, Paul wants to show the vivid contrast between spiritual gifts exercised **with love**, and spiritual gifts exercised **without love**.

The *"more excellent way"* then, is certainly not to claim love at the expense of spiritual gifts, nor spiritual gifts at the expense of love, but rather to reach out for and use the charismata only within an environment of love.

Some people say, "Love is the most important gift"; but nowhere is love called a gift. Others say, "We need a baptism of love"; but love is never called a baptism. It is incorrect to compare love with the baptism in the Holy Spirit, or with the gifts of the Holy Spirit; love is complementary to these things, not antagonistic to them.

Do you want the Holy Spirit to see in you a fit vessel through which to manifest one or more of his supernatural gifts? Then follow Paul's *"more excellent way"* of love. Love should be the motivating force behind all yearning for spiritual gifts; love should clothe with beauty every exercise of the charismata.

Paul could not encourage the Corinthians to *"desire the higher gifts"* while ignoring the need for Christian love; nor could he tell them to *"follow after love"* while despising spiritual gifts. He presented to them rather the more excellent way of coveting the best gifts while simultaneously following after love.

So the alternatives that are set before the believer are not gifts or love, nor good works or love, but rather gifts and good works - **with love** or **without love**. The choice is ours. [a]

---

[a] Note: if it is true, as some claim, that Paul was urging the Corinthians to discard the charismata, especially glossolalia, in favour of love, then we must also say that he was telling them to discard prophecy, understanding, knowledge, faith, acts of charity, and martyrdom! (13:1-3)

(B) PROFITLESS GIFTS

It is difficult for many people to accept that the gifts of the Spirit are subject to corruption. Yet the apostle lists a wide variety of gifts and works that may be displayed without love, which makes them profitless to their users (13:1-3).

A believer may -

"speak with the tongues of men and of angels"
"have the gift of prophecy"
"may understand all mysteries" (words of wisdom*)*
"may understand all knowledge" (the word of knowledge)
"may have all faith"
"may give away all he has to feed the poor"
"may give his body to be burned"
- but, if those things are done without love as his or her motive and aim, then that believer becomes...

"a noisy gong and a clanging cymbal"
"as nothing"
"without gain."
Notice carefully that Paul does not call the gifts and ministries of the Spirit profitless. Would it be claimed that giving many goods to the poor, or suffering martyrdom, has no value? Consider this:

- ♦ if a man gives all his goods to feed the poor, it will certainly profit the poor;
- ♦ if he gives his body to be burned, his witness might inspire many others;
- ♦ if he prophesies, those who hear him might receive benefit;
- ♦ if he moves mountains by faith, great advantage might come to the church;
- ♦ if he communicates the wisdom and knowledge of God the people might be well-instructed.

But if he himself lacks love, his gifts and his good works will bring ***him*** no reward.

Notice that Paul portrays *himself* here: *"though I speak ... "* The great apostle experienced every manifestation of the Spirit, and he heartily praised God for it. Yet he said that if he used the charismata without love even he would be nothing. His gift might benefit other people, but it would bring *him* no profit.

This rule is especially true of glossolalia. Other gifts of the Spirit, even when they are exercised without love, may retain value for the church; but loveless glossolalia is emptied of all supernatural grace. Lacking divine love, glossolalia benefits neither the hearers nor the speaker, becoming as unpleasant as a *"cracked gong or a jarring cymbal"*. Despite the absence of love, other gifts may retain their character as manifestations of the Holy Spirit. But glossolalia stripped of love no longer possesses any true spiritual character.[a]

Another fact also appears. Lack of love eventually causes any gift or ministry to wither away. Think about Samson. He was a mighty warrior for the Lord and for Israel; the Spirit was strong in his life. How well he loved God! How well he served Israel! But his virtue was consumed by his lust for Delilah. For a long time, though Samson persisted in sin, the Lord remained patient with him. But inevitably the day came when the Holy Spirit withdrew, *"and Samson did not know that the Lord had left him"* (Jg 16:20).

The same was true of King Saul. His constant failure to walk righteously before the Lord, his determination to hate rather than love, led to an inexorable doom: *"The Spirit of the Lord departed from Saul, and an evil spirit from the Lord tormented him"* (1 Sa 16:14).

But perhaps the most outstanding example of this principle is found in the man who had one of the greatest prophetic gifts of all time - Balaam. Of him it is said -

[a] See the last chapter of this book for a fuller discussion of the special nature of glossolalia as an utterance of the human spirit.

"the Lord put a word in his mouth" (Nu 23:5)
"the Lord met Balaam" (vs. 16)
"the Spirit of God came upon him" (24:2)

- and his oracles were the words of

"the man whose eye is opened" (vs. 3)
"him who hears the words of God" (vs. 4)
"him who sees the vision of the Almighty" (vs. 4)
"him who spoke what God spoke" (vs. 12)
"him who knows the knowledge of the Most High"
(vs. 16)

Balaam's oracles were accurately fulfilled in Israel and in Christ. His prophetic words have brought blessing and inspiration to millions of people. His predictions are still being accomplished, with worldwide ramifications. Universal history has been shaped by the unfolding of his visions about Israel and the nations, and about the Deliverer and King who was to come. But because he was motivated by greed and sought to deceive God's people, his life ended wretchedly. He was put to death as a common criminal (Nu 31:16; Js 13:22; 2 Pe 2:15; Ju 11). His revelations benefited others; but they profited *him* nothing. He lost both his gift and his life. His fate should warn us that our motive for seeking and exercising the charismata must be one of love - love for the honour of God and of the church.

Love is known by the good it produces. Love that exists only to get is not love, but greed. True love continually strives to give rather than to receive joy. Love finds ultimate satisfaction only in giving. It follows the pattern set by God, who *"so* loved that he *gave"*. That quality of giving, self-sacrificing love should be the strong motivating force of our lives. Every word and action should be decided and directed by love.

The apostle lists the distinguishing marks of this divine love. They are the fruit of the Spirit of Christ in the believer (13:4-8). We notice that

- true love is not an emotion; rather it is an attitude, an outlook
- it does not consist of feeling, but of character
- it does not necessarily require us to *like* somebody.

Actually, a demand to "like" everyone, that is, to have affectionate feelings toward all humanity, would be impossible to fulfil. Yet we can, by divine grace, **love** every man and woman. For example, it will hardly be supposed that Jesus "liked" the Pharisees (cp. Mt 23:13-26); yet it cannot be denied that he *loved* them - for Calvary embraces them as well as all other people. Jesus demonstrated his love, not by feelings, but by actions.

Hence not one of the characteristics of love listed by Paul requires emotion. Each term he used denotes rather a disposition, or a pattern of behaviour. They show that we are to love others as God loves us, which he began to do even while we were still his enemies (Ro 5:8).

Suppose a drunken tramp were to come knocking on your door, pleading for help. You probably would not feel any fondness for him. In fact, his filth, his stink, his degradation, might well repulse you. But with the love of God in your heart, you could still welcome him into your home and help him. Later, if he responded to your aid, you might grow to love him, not just as a Christian but as a dear brother. But whether or not you and I ever become fond of our neighbours, we nonetheless owe a debt of godly love to all, whether they are friends or foes.

This, then, is the kind of love that should motivate and undergird our association with the gifts of the Holy Spirit.

Against such a background as that the charismata will shine with splendid lustre and will be immensely profitable both to those who use them and to the church.

Notice, though, that *"making love your aim"* will not by itself produce charismata in the church. The command does not end there, for Paul continues: *"earnestly desire spiritual gifts"* (1 Co 14:1). A true balance can be maintained only when due emphasis is given to both commands. To seek spiritual gifts apart from a love-motive, is to court carnality and disaster. But to follow after love and ignore the charismata, is to deprive the church of things that put divine muscle into its work. The nine-fold *charismata* of the Spirit (1 Co 12:8-10), and the nine-fold *fruit* of the Spirit (Ga 5:22), are equally necessary if the full *glory* of the Spirit is to be seen in the church.

(II) THEY MUST BE EXERCISED IN FAITH

The rule applies here as to any other part of Christian experience: *"Without faith it is impossible to please God"* (He 11:6). In other words, Spirit-filled Christians should be so walking in the Spirit, and so living in conformity with the Father's will, that whenever they need a particular gift of the Spirit they can immediately trust God for its appearance.

That is how I understand the instruction, *"earnestly desire the best gifts"* (1 Co 12:31). Notice that the word "gifts" is plural. This suggests to me, not that we should plead for weeks on end for a certain gift, nor that we should single out one gift as inherently better than another, but rather that we should be open to *all* the charismata. Then, as each occasion arises, we should specifically grasp whatever gift (or gifts) will bring the best gain to us and to the church.

As I walk in the Spirit day by day, I should maintain a general desire that the Holy Spirit will equip me for God's service by imparting to me whatever charismata my work demands. Then, as some particular need appears, I will be able at once to unleash faith, confidently expecting the Spirit to endow me freely with those gifts that each changing situation requires.

(III) THEY MUST BE EXERCISED UNDER AUTHORITY

Paul disallows any charismatic gift to hold authority over either scripture or the church. On the contrary, he insists that all "pneumatika" (whether persons or manifestations, ministries or gifts) must function within biblical boundaries and remain under the authority of the church. The charismata are set in the church for the benefit of the church. The Spirit imparts them to *"up-build, encourage, console, edify, and bring learning to"* the church. If they fail in this purpose, if they speak against scripture, if they create confusion, or dishonour Christ, then they must be called disorderly, and the church must bring them under discipline (1 Co 12:3; 14:12,29,33,37-40; 1 Th 5:21).

Name that church "Folly!" which allows itself to be so carried away with awe of spiritual gifts, or with enthusiasm for them, that it refuses to control their exercise. Within a framework of authority and discipline, the charismata can operate freely in the church to its great profit. But if control of the gifts is relaxed, confusion and carnality, deception and disruption will soon result.

In this connection 1 Co 14:13-20 is an important passage. Christians who reserve their main enthusiasm for spiritual gifts, who resent any restraint being placed either upon them or their gifts, are like little children chasing after baubles and ignoring things of deeper value (vs. 20). Now there are some things in which we should indeed be like babies, innocent and ingenuous. When evil beckons, let us remain altogether without guile. But toward the church and its worship we should show mature understanding (vs. 20).

That is why Paul, much as he enjoyed the pleasures of glossolalia (vs. 18,14), was more determined to utilise fully his rational faculties. He would gladly *"pray with the spirit"*; but he placed equal emphasis on *"praying with the mind"* (vs. 15). A spiritually barren intellectualism, and an intellectually barren spiritualism were equally repulsive to Paul.

So the apostle to preserve a balance between both aspects of worship: the rational and the spiritual. Indeed, dare we call worship truly Christian unless both are present? But always final authority rested with "mature thinking", not with spontaneous or ecstatic outbursts, nor with uncontrolled emotionalism. Against this rule, and against the authority of scripture, Paul would brook no opposition; no matter how mighty or how spiritual the "prophet" might seem to be (vs. 37-38).

Chapter Seven

PAUL'S SERMON

The gifts of the Holy Spirit have a particular place in the church, and a particular relationship to other ministries that function there. Ignorance of the proper use of the charismata has led to much wrong thinking, wrong seeking, and wrong practice. That was the case in apostolic times, just as it is today. Paul was unwilling to tolerate that ignorance, so he wrote the three chapters that are the major text for this book, 1 Corinthians 12, 13, and 14. A portion of his instructions seems to be a precis of one of his own sermons (12:4-31). The passage has a formal structure, which consists of a text, three sections of comment, and a conclusion. Out of this apostolic sermon comes a magnificent revelation of the nature of the church, of the special relationship to the church held by each member of the Godhead, and of the place occupied in the church by the charismata.

THE GODHEAD AND THE CHARISMATA

INTRODUCTION

Paul's intention was magnificent. He gave himself the task of showing how the entire Godhead actively relates to the church, and how Father, Son and Holy Spirit work in perfect harmony to fulfil the divine purpose for the church. Nothing, therefore, that destroys this unity of purpose and of achievement, can claim to be a genuine gift or ministry. Whatever contradicts the will of God, no matter how supernatural it may be, cannot possibly come from God.

Furthermore, Paul argues that we have a duty, not to focus our attention on spiritual gifts, but rather to view those gifts in the light of the over-all purpose of God. True gifts of the *Spirit*, since they are set in the church, will always conform to the operations of the *Father*, and the *Son* in the church.

Now we come to Paul's three-fold text and to his enlargement of each part -

Text:

> *"There are varieties of gifts, but the same Spirit; and there are varieties of ministry, but the same Lord; and there are varieties of working, but the same God" (vs. 4-6).*

(A) VARIETIES OF GIFTS

> *"There are varieties of gifts, but the same Spirit" (vs. 4).*

You will find Paul's comment on that part of his text in vs. 7-11.

The Holy Spirit brings into the church, and makes available to every member of the church, various supernatural endowments. These spiritual manifestations are given to enable the church to carry on the actual ministry begun by Christ himself (Jn 14:12; Mk 16:15-20). In practice the Holy Spirit will *"divide"* the gifts according to his own will. Hence the separation or uniting of the gifts, their distribution and the measure in which they are given, remain under the sovereign control of the Spirit. Note also that the choice of the Spirit in giving a gift will always be made in harmony with the purpose of the Father and the Son.

Further, the gifts are *"worked"* by the Spirit, not by the people. The word is *"energeo"*, and it means to be "active" or "efficient". Apart from the anointing and dynamic energising of the Spirit no spiritual gift can accomplish its rightful purpose. What is that purpose? Nothing less than to bring profit, both to the user and to the church, and to produce in the church unity, not schism.

This, then, is the relationship of the Holy Spirit to the church: he endows the church with supernatural equipment, and then energises that equipment by his own presence and power, so that the church may work the works of Christ in the world.

(B) VARIETIES OF MINISTRY

> *"There are varieties of ministry, but the same Lord"*
> *(vs. 5).*

You will find Paul's comment on that part of his text in vs. 12-27.

Christ, who is the Creator and Designer of the human body (Cl 1:16-18) has also designed and created the church. This church was established to provide a framework in which both the *"ministries"* (or "ministry gifts", Ep 4:11) of Christ and the manifestations of the Spirit could operate. Christ patterned the church on the human body; hence the church is called "body" of Christ, of which he is the "head".

We can pull at least four lessons out of the apostle's illustration of the human body:

- ◆ the members of our bodies are quite unlike each other, and they all have separate and unique functions
- ◆ nonetheless they all make up one body, which is controlled by the head, the seat of our mind and will
- ◆ all the members of our bodies act in harmony with each other and with the whole body - in fact, they can stay alive, and perform properly, only when they function, not for their own benefit, but for the benefit of the entire body
- ◆ the members of our bodies are not interchangeable; their positions and functions are irrevocably ordained by the will of the Designer.

The church is the body of Christ. Christ is the head, the creative and controlling Authority of that church. Believers are the members of that body, each diverse, each with a separate function, each with different talents and abilities, each expected to work in harmony with all the others to the happiness and well-being of the whole church.

This then is the relationship of Christ to the church - he is its architect and head.

(C) VARIETIES OF WORKING

"There are varieties of working, but it is the same God" (vs. 6)

You will find Paul's comment on that part of his text in vs. 27-30.

In this passage we learn that the actual placing of the members into the "body" is the prerogative of the Father. Christ created the church and designated himself as its Head: but the building of each individual member into the church is wrought by God. To the Father belongs the disposal and final outworking of every gift and every ministry to secure the proper health and balance of the church and its work.

Just as Jesus carefully and distinctly chose the twelve disciples, knowing that they were "given" to him by the Father (Jn 6:39), so today also God, by his own will and perfect knowledge of every factor, chooses various people for various tasks *("varieties or working")* within the whole church.

Thus, since Christ has created the basic pattern of the church, with its designated offices and functions *("diakonia"* = "administrations"), God may now appoint each individual to his or her rightful service in the church. These "workers" are particularised as those who fulfil the various tasks of the "members of the body"; viz. *"apostles, prophets, teachers, workers of miracles, healers, helpers, administrators, speakers in various kinds of tongues"* etc.

This then is the relationship of the Father to the church - he places into the various positions in the church those whom he chooses by his own sovereign will.

Paul's vision is daring and breathtaking. He brings the entire Godhead into relationship with the church. We should try to catch the same vision, and to cooperate with it, which means that we should -

(1) recognise the ministries Christ has created and that we are each suited to one or more of them;

(2) acknowledge the unity and cooperation of Father, Son, and Holy Spirit in their activity in the church, and merge ourselves with this divine partnership, recognising that

- the **Father** never places the wrong person in a ministry, office, or function in the church; and that

- the **Son** does not remove a God-placed believer from the church, nor change the proper office each person should hold; and that

- the **Spirit** will not give the wrong gift to any person, nor withhold the right one.

CONCLUSIONS

(1) The church, designed and created by Christ, is his "body" on earth, and we are all members of that "body".

(2) However, we have actually been placed in the church by God (Jn 6:44), by whose selection we have each been given a particular role to fulfil in the church.

(3) Hence, some are apostles, some are prophets, others are teachers, helpers, administrators, pastors, and so on.

(4) Similarly, into the church the Holy Spirit has brought various endowments (the charismata) that are designed to equip the various ministry gifts of Christ, so that those ministers may fulfil their tasks with divine power and efficiency.

(5) Are all believers, apostles, or teachers, or pastors, or evangelists, or deacons, or prophets, etc.? Of course not - for just as the members of our physical bodies vary in their appointed functions and hence in their endowments, so do the "members" of the "body" of Christ. An eye is endowed with the faculty of sight, not of hearing; an ear has the faculty of hearing, not of speaking; and so on.

(6) Therefore, since all are not apostles, or prophets, or teachers, etc., neither do all have the gift of healing, or of working miracles, or of wisdom, or of speaking in tongues, etc. Each ministry, office, function, in the body of Christ requires its own special spiritual gift (or gifts).

(7) This means that all Spirit-filled Christians are faced with the solemn responsibility of soberly assessing their position in the church, and then of earnestly coveting those charismata that are necessary to fulfil that position properly. That is the meaning of Paul's injunction: *"earnestly desire the best gifts"* (vs. 31). It may be stated simply as: *"the best gifts are those that best suit the requirements of my present position and task in the church, the body of Christ."*

DESIRE SPIRITUAL GIFTS

INTRODUCTION

Further commentary on what it means to *"desire"* the gifts of the Spirit can be found in Romans 12:1-8. There Paul again surprisingly mixes together a collection of ordinary and extraordinary abilities. We should remind ourselves once more to avoid the error of making any sharp distinction between natural and supernatural skills; except to say that natural gifts are useful to God only as they are suffused by the Holy Spirit.

(A) LAYING A GOOD FOUNDATION

The finest foundation for ministry, and for receiving the gifts of the Spirit, begins with full surrender to the will of God: *"I appeal to you ... present your bodies as a living sacrifice, holy and acceptable to God"* (vs. 1). Here is where all seeking after spiritual gifts must begin. The charismata are available, and operate, not according to human will, but only *"as the Spirit wills"* (1 Co 12:11). We can expect a free flow of the charismata in our own lives only through the channel of total surrender to God.

However, merely to yield to the divine will is not sufficient by itself to produce charismata. Many Christians are deeply committed to God, yet have no experience of spiritual gifts. A yielded life must be accompanied by an attitude of mind that does not accept the limitations of the world. Rather, it must lift itself into that realm of the Spirit where the supernatural works of God are the accepted norm (Ro 12:2a - *"do not be conformed to this world, but be transformed by the renewal of your mind."*[a]

Are you surrendered to the will of God? Then you should remember also that the divine will includes a flow of charismata. Therefore you should use your faith in God to obtain whatever gifts are consonant with the call you have received.

The special aim of this life-surrender and mind-renewal is two-fold -

(1) *"to prove what is the will of God"* (that is, to discover the ministry or work God has given you in the church); and hence

(2) to prove *"what is good and acceptable and perfect"* (that is, to discover which of the charismata are available to you, and when and how they should be exercised).

---

[a] Remember 1 Co 12:1, and Paul's reference to *"pneumatika"*.

(B) CHARISMATA AND THE GRACE OF GOD

Paul says that *"we have gifts that differ according to the grace given to us"* and that these are the gifts we must *"use"* (vs. 6). We are first given *"grace"*; and after that, *"gifts"*.

So before we can determine what gifts we can use, we must decide what grace we have been given, for the gifts are dependent upon this grace. What is this "grace"? I would like to suggest four things -

(1) NATURAL ABILITY

We are all born with certain natural gifts and abilities. They play a large part in the work God appoints for us in the church, and hence in the gifts we can receive and use. The varying degrees of natural ability each person has been given will result in different callings and charismata.

The parable of the talents well illustrates this, especially Jesus' words: *"to each according to his ability"* (Mat 25:14-30). Here are three men receiving a job to do, and equipment for that job, according to their capacity to handle it. One man was given five talents, another two talents, and the third only one. The man with five talents was no more favoured than the others. Commensurate with their abilities, they were each given the same proportion of talents and were each offered an equal reward. God knows the aptitude of each person, and he usually gives us, first, work to do that fits our skills, and then spiritual gifts to suit that work. In the parable, the *"talents"* represent a combination of both *opportunity* for service and *endowment* for service combined. In other words, they join both "work" and "gifts" together, laid upon a foundation of natural proficiency.

Notice also that reward is not based on greatness of opportunity, nor upon greatness of achievement, but only upon faithfulness in making full use of whatever opportunity God has given. The man with five talents used them wisely, and doubled his investment. So also did the man with two talents. To both of them their employer gave an identical reward: *"Well done, good and faithful servant; you have been faithful over a little, I will set you over much; enter into the joy of your lord"* (vs. 21,23). But contrast that with the master's anger against the man who buried his talent (vs. 26-30).

(2) SPIRITUAL ABILITY

> *"(Think about yourself) according to the measure of faith that God has assigned to you" (vs. 3b).*

For the purpose of this study, let me paraphrase Paul's *"assigned measure of faith"* to read *"the ability released in you by the new birth"*. If our natural birth brought to us certain natural abilities, then I suggest that our spiritual birth has brought to us certain spiritual abilities; and the measure of spiritual ability we have each received is as diverse as our different natural abilities. Not all have the same spiritual capacity; not all are attracted by the same spiritual goals; not all share the same spiritual emphases; not all respond to the same spiritual stimuli; not all have the same spiritual awareness, or sensitivity, or strength, or genius - we are as personally unique, as truly individual and unlike each other *spiritually*, as we are naturally.[a]

So it is just as foolish to force people to be identical spiritually as it is to force them to be identical naturally. Some are spiritually strong, others weaker; some are highly creative spiritually, others less so; some have great spiritual genius, others almost none. None of us

---

[a] For example, note the two different men described by Paul in 1 Co 7:36-38. One had little control over his sexual drive; the other was sternly in command of himself. Paul did not criticise the weaker and commend the stronger. He acknowledged the reality that we are not all the same, and he prescribed a different remedy for each man. How unlike many modern pious evangelicals and pentecostals that is! They would insist that anyone, by properly using the means of grace, can rise to the highest heights of spiritual grace and victory. Paul was more down to earth.

should be disturbed by this, nor envious of others, nor scornful of them, any more than we are when they have greater or lesser natural abilities than we have. Those who are wise accept themselves as they are. They set themselves to discover what has been born in them, and then to develop those abilities as fully as they can.

Realise then that the limitations placed on our *spiritual* abilities by the accidents of the new birth are parallel to, and as final as, the limitations placed on our *natural* abilities by the accidents of physical birth.

Let me illustrate. I have some small skill as piano player. Sometimes when I have been tickling the ivories an idle thought has crossed my mind that it would be enormous fun to be a concert pianist. However, no matter how hard I try, or how long I practise, the limitations forced on me by temperament, physical development, muscular flexibility, and scant musical gift, forever prevent me from fulfilling that wild dream! I lack an inherent genius. So I am content to own a nice upright piano that was given to me by a dear friend. To buy me a glorious Steinway would be a dreadful waste! Who gives a learner violinist a Stradivarius?

Likewise, spiritually, I have been "born again" with a certain inherent spiritual capacity. The restraints imposed by the boundaries of that capacity limit both the additional gifts I can receive from God and the extent to which I can exercise them. God is no more likely to press me into a situation that is not commensurate with who and what I am, than an entrepreneur is likely to invite to me to perform as a celebrity piano soloist.

(3) THE PROPORTION OF FAITH

Paul says that we can *"use (the charismata) ... (only) in proportion to our faith"* (vs. 6). I take this to mean "according to the measure of our spiritual development at the time of use." In other words, at any given time you and I have reached a certain point of spiritual growth and development, our faith has reached a certain strength, our spiritual capacity has developed just so far. Those factors place a definite ceiling on the heights we can reach in the reception and exercise of the charismata. My responsibility is to know what I am just now, to fulfil my ministry, and to use the charismata within the limits of what I am - which does not prevent me from continually waiting on God for an extension of those limits.

So I cannot go beyond the "proportion of faith" into which I have grown at any time. Nonetheless, I should certainly press to the limits of that proportion, and do all that I can to promote its increase. But for now, this "proportion of faith" (that is, the limits placed on me by my present spiritual development) will determine the charismata that are available to me and the measure to which I can use them.

(4) A PARTICULAR CALLING

> *"In each human body there are various limbs, which all have different functions. Similarly, although we are many, we yet comprise one body in Christ, and we all belong to each other as its members." (vs. 4-5).*

Just as each member of the human body must be endowed with unique skills, so must each member of the church, the body of Christ. That is why Paul says, *"we have gifts that differ one from another"*. Therefore the Holy Spirit divides the charismata among the members of the church in exact accordance with the ministry-gifts each member has received from Christ.

So, some may be apostles, with a profusion of charismata; while others are "helpers" with perhaps only one spiritual gift. Each calling, each ministry, each form of Christian service, has its own associated charismata that we should ask for and use to the limits of the grace God has given us.

In the meantime we must continually remind ourselves that if the church is to function in perfect harmony and truly to fulfil the purpose of God, then every member of the "body" is essential. We must avoid the fault of being ashamed because our gifts and calling seem to be less important than those of other members of the body do; and also avoid the even more hateful fault of scorning those who seem to have a lesser grace than we have received.

We should recognise that we all have a set position in the body of Christ, that the body is not dependent upon us for life, but we are dependent upon the body. The members of the human body can function only as they function for the benefit of the whole body. The eye has sight in it, but it can see only as it remains in harmonious union with the body, in its proper place, and works for the benefit of the body. If it does otherwise it will soon lose its gift of sight.

Likewise, you have a certain function to fulfil within the church, the body of Christ, and there are certain charismata especially available to you to enable you to fulfil that function. If you are occupying your proper place in the body then you may (and should) reach out for and use the charismata that belong to that position, always using every gift for the benefit of the body and the glory of God.

(C) GRASPING THE PROMISE

Against that background of grace, Paul's gives a series of instructions-

(1) We must maintain a *"sober judgment"* (vs. 3); which means that we are not to have either too high or too low an opinion of ourselves. Both faults are equally hurtful to the good progress of the work of God. Without *"sober judgment"* a person will either be puffed up with pride and will venture where God has not called; or, thinking too humbly, will shrink back from tasks that God has appointed. Possibly one of the most urgent needs among Christian people is to face themselves honestly, to know who they are, what they are, what they can do, and what they cannot do.

(2) We must set ourselves to know the calling God has given us. Is it *"to prophesy, to serve, to teach, to exhort, to contribute, to give aid, to show mercy"* (vs. 6-8)? All these and many other forms of service have been created by Christ in the church. Into one or more of them God has placed each of us. Let us be content with the form of service God has appointed for us, and devote ourselves to the best of our ability to fulfilling the divine mandate. To do anything else is folly, and serves only to disrupt the smooth functioning of the *"body"*. Can the eye function as an ear, or the hand as a foot?

(3) We must earnestly desire those spiritual gifts that are "best" for the position we hold in the body of Christ. To an eye belongs the gift of seeing, and to an ear the gift of hearing. Of what use is hearing to the eye, or seeing to the ear? In fact, the eye can "hear" only through the ear, and the ear can "see" only through the eye. So all the parts of our bodies work together for their collective benefit, each fulfilling its function by utilising those gifts that are peculiar to it. That is how it should it be in the church, the body of Christ.

(4) We may not in any way envy one another, nor behave proudly in each other's presence. Rather, *"Let your love be utterly sincere, hate what is evil, and hold fast to what is good. Love each other as true brothers should; esteem your fellow Christians more than you esteem yourself. Never let your zeal wilt, stay ardent in the Spirit, serve the Lord"* (vs. 9-11).

(D) CONCLUSION

To conclude this chapter on the position of the charismata in the church, here is a general summary:

(1) We must study the nine-fold gifts of the Holy Spirit, and know their value and purpose - it is a shame to be ignorant of these things.

(2) We must have a sober evaluation of ourselves, not thinking ourselves to be what we are not, nor coveting a position in the church other than what God has fitted each of us for.

(3) We have different gifts and different faith, but let us use what we have wisely and well and we shall all gain an equal reward.

(4) The gifts of the Spirit, while they may function in any believer at any time of need, are particularly associated with various ministries. Each ministry and gift that comes from God will work in harmony with the whole body of Christ. Those things that come from the Holy Spirit may be recognised by the unity they bring to the church, and the fruit they bear for the Lord.

(5) While we are each called to a particular ministry in the church, those ministries cannot become fully effective unless they are anointed and empowered by the charismata.

(6) So, knowing the purpose of the gifts of the Holy Spirit, and knowing our respective functions within the body of Christ, let us covet earnestly the gift or gifts that are best suited to us.

(7) But always remember that, unlike our mortal bodies, the church, which is the body of Christ, is not static. The church is constantly changing; each believer's position in relation to the body of Christ may be altered. As our faith and experience grow we are brought to positions where greater service is required of us. Of this we must be continually aware, always having a proper estimation of our calling, always coveting those gifts that at the present moment are best.

And, as Paul said, *"Having gifts ... let us use them!"*

Chapter Eight

SPEAKING OUT!

Paul was certainly determined to banish the ignorance of the Corinthians! So far he has shown the general nature of the charismata and their place in the church (1 Co 12). Then he insisted upon the supreme importance of love as the only proper framework in which to use the charismata (1 Co 13). Then he brought this part of his discussion to a close with the words, *"Make love your aim, and earnestly desire spiritual gifts, but especially that you may prophesy"* (14:1).

But he is not yet done. For now he moves into a discussion of the relative merits and the proper use of the three gifts of utterance: *prophecy, speaking in tongues, and interpretation of tongues.*

Let us recognise at once that the phrase *"especially that you may prophesy"* does not mean that prophecy is always the best of the charismata. Such a claim would contradict what he has taught in the previous two chapters. Rather it means only that prophecy is preferable to glossolalia, particularly in the context of serving the church (cp. vs. 5, where the same statement - identical in Greek - *"but even more to prophesy"*, is repeated in direct contrast with speaking in tongues).

Paul draws the contrast a second time when he writes: *"someone who prophesies is greater than someone who speaks in tongues"* (vs. 5). And that this comparison is true only within the limited context of ministering to the church is shown by vs. 18-19 (where the same Greek word is used again): *"I thank God that I speak in tongues more than all of you do; yet <u>in church</u> I would rather speak five words with* *my mind, so that I might teach others, than ten thousand words in a tongue".*

So the comparison is not one of prophecy versus the remaining charismata; nor even one of prophecy versus glossolalia; but rather prophecy versus glossolalia when they occur during a church meeting. In another context any one of the other charismata, including glossolalia, might be more useful than prophecy - for example, outside the task of instructing the church, Paul emphatically declared; *"I thank God that I speak in tongues more than (the same Greek word again!) any of you do!".*

The comparative adverb used by Paul in each of those places *("mallon")* need not have the force of absolute opposition. It often means only *"more than"* - e.g. Mt 18:13; Ro 8:34; 1 Co 9:12; 2 Pe 1:10, etc. That is the sense in which Paul uses *mallon* in 1 Co 14:1,4,19. He is not urging them to scrap glossolalia in favour of prophecy. On the contrary, he is saying, *"I want you to desire spiritual gifts; I want you to speak in tongues; but even more than this (especially when you speak to the church) I want you to use the gift of prophecy".*

The reason for this preference for prophecy as a ministry to the church is obvious (vs. 2-4):

On the one hand: "Those who speak in other tongues do not speak to other people, but to God." The glossolalist edifies himself or herself.

On the other hand: "Someone who prophesies speaks to the church ... to strengthen the people, and to encourage and comfort them." The prophet edifies the church.

However, the position is altered when an utterance in glossolalia is followed by an interpretation: *"Someone who prophesies is greater than someone who speaks in tongues, unless someone else interprets, so that the church may be edified"* (vs. 5b). The preposition "unless" expresses an important exception, for it shows that the twin gifts of "tongues and interpretation" are equal in value to the gift of prophecy, and serve the same purpose: to **"edify"** the church. How could it be otherwise? Paul cannot criticise or condemn glossolalia itself, for it is a genuine manifestation of the Holy Spirit. Paul himself used glossolalia extravagantly (vs. 18). His criticism and restraints are not directed against the Spirit's gift, but against the wrongful practice of the Corinthians.

(A) SOME INTERESTING SUGGESTIONS

Now I would like to digress a little, and look at some alternative suggestions or objections that have been raised about these matters.

(1) FIRST SUGGESTION

Some have suggested that all glossolalia is addressed to God (vs. 2), never to people; therefore it is wrong to use the gift to address the church, as if it were a message from God. A corollary arises from that suggestion: if glossolalia is either a prayer to God, or an act of worship and praise, then interpretation of tongues will be either *(a)* a rendering into the vernacular of the contents of that prayer or worship; or *(b)* perhaps even a divine answer to the prayer, or response to the praise. In either case, the interpretation will not be in the form of a prophetic message to the church.

Now, I do not doubt that glossolalia spoken aloud in the church may be a prayer or an act of praise, and that the interpretation should convey that meaning to the people. But to say that it must *always* be so seems too rigid. Paul indicates clearly enough that glossolalia (linked with interpretation) may be addressed prophetically to the church:

(a) See vs. 27-28. When no *"interpreter"* is present, the glossolalist must speak only *"to himself* (that is, softly) *and to God"* - he or she can still use the gift in praise and worship, but not in such a way as to command the attention of the church. By contrast, when there is an *"interpreter"* in the meeting, the glossolalist may speak, not quietly, nor just to God, but to the church, in the form of a prophetic message.

(b) See vs. 5, which shows that tongues and interpretation serve the same basic purpose as prophecy, namely, to edify the church.

(c) Paul plainly says that he is free to speak to the church in tongues, providing his glossolalia is rendered into the vernacular (vs. 6). The verse could be paraphrased: *"If I came to you speaking in tongues, what benefit would you gain unless, through interpretation, I brought you some revelation, or knowledge, or prophecy, or teaching?"* Notice that interpretation of tongues may embrace the *word of wisdom* ("revelation"), the *word of knowledge*, the gift of *prophecy*, and *teaching*. It may also take the form of prayer and of "blessing" God (vs. 15-16). Surely then it is unnecessarily restrictive to say that interpretation of tongues must always be couched in the form of prayer, praise, exhortation, or any other fixed form?

(d) The suggestion that interpretation of tongues is God's response to a prayer uttered in glossolalia hardly does justice to the meaning of the word *"interpretation"*. It is not an interpretation of the mind of God, but an interpretation of the tongue. The Greek word is *"diarmeneuo"* = to interpret fully, to explain, to expound the meaning of something. When applied to a glossolalic utterance it can reasonably mean only that the sense and significance of the glossolalic words are being put into the vernacular speech of the church.

However, my comments below on the vocal gifts arising from the human spirit will show that any rendering of glossolalia into the vernacular should not be viewed as parallel to, say, turning Greek into English. The latter involves two natural languages, both intelligible to the human mind, and both arising from the mind. But the former (interpretation of tongues) involves one intelligible language, and one unintelligible language, [a]but both of them arising from *the human spirit* (not the mind).

(2) SECOND SUGGESTION

It is sometimes taught, on the basis of vs. 13, that glossolalists should pray for, and then deliver, an interpretation of their own speaking in tongues. Some have even suggested that tongues and interpretation can become a kind of personal dialogue between the person and God. The glossolalist addresses God in tongues; and then God replies, using the glossolalist's voice to speak an interpretation of that tongue. Concerning this I would suggest –

(a) Paul insists that tongues and interpretation, when linked together, are given to edify the *church*, not the individual. They are limited to two or at the most three occurrences (vs. 27), and they must be judged *by the church* (vs. 29). Those requirements surely preclude any private use of interpretation (and of prophecy).

(b) Paul's injunction concerning *"interpreters"* (vs. 27,28) requires an interpreter other than the person who spoke in tongues.

(c) But what about the instruction in vs. 13 - *"anyone who speaks in a tongue should pray for the power to interpret"*? - see also vs. 13. The same verb occurs in both places. Normal Greek usage would assume that the subject of the clause is the glossolalist - in which case, the verb would be rendered *"he should interpret"* (vs. 5), and *"he may interpret"* (vs. 13). However (even if it is awkward), because the verb is in the subjunctive mood a different translation is possible: *"unless someone interprets ... pray for someone to*

---

[a] Glossolalia may or may not consist of a known language. Usually no human language of any kind is involved in glossolalia. But sometimes, as on the Day of Pentecost, either a vocal miracle or an auditory one may be superimposed onto glossolalia speech.

interpret." [a]Essentially, the subject of the verb is unspecified; it may be the glossolalist, or it may be another. Only the context can decide the question; and it seems to me that Paul's distinction between those who speak in tongues and those who interpret forces the subject of "interpret" to be someone other than the glossolalist (cp. 12:10, 30; 14:27-28).

Hence the statements in vs. 5,13 simply require that a person who wishes to exercise the gift of tongues in the church should pray for God to raise up others with the gift of interpretation.

It must be allowed, of course, that people with the gift of tongues can also receive and use the gift of interpretation, and at times it may be necessary for them to interpret their own tongues messages (cp. vs. 6). But as a general rule the church should expect someone other than the glossolalist to bring an interpretation.

(3) THIRD SUGGESTION

Someone may now ask: "If tongues and interpretation serve the same general purpose as prophecy, why not dispense with one of these gifts? At least one of them seems to be redundant."

To which I would reply -

(a) Paul said that the Holy Spirit brings *"varieties"* of gifts into the church (12:4). Much of the beauty of these gifts lies in their diversity. The interchange of tongues and interpretation with prophecy adds to the worship of the church and to the ministry of the Spirit a richness that one gift alone could not provide. In any case, to complain that God is bestowing on his church too many treasures suggests a parsimonious mind and a narrow vision.

---

[a] That rendering is supported by the NRSV (verse 5), the TEV (verse 5), and others.

(b) Paul states three principles that govern the way in which the charismata are spread around the church (Ro 12:3,6):

♦ how much grace we have received from God
♦ what measure of faith has been given to us
♦ what level of faith we have reached.

Some, then, have enough grace and faith to receive and use, say the gift of tongues; but to address the church in prophecy lies beyond their capacity. They find it much easier to speak out in glossolalia, where the mind is inactive, than to speak in prophecy or interpretation, where the mind, as well as the spirit, is involved.

Others find they can deliver a prophecy, but are deterred from interpretation. They are fearful that their faith might not rise to the level of unction displayed in a powerful and anointed message in tongues.

The existence of three gifts of utterance makes it possible for the greatest number of Spirit-filled believers to take an active and vocal part in the worship of the church.

(c) Paul says that the gift of tongues serves the special purpose of providing a *"sign to unbelievers"* (14:22); hence it has a unique function that prophecy alone does not fulfil.

(d) Prophecy by itself, since it is spoken in the vernacular, is always open to criticism. It may be simply a cleverly contrived speech rather than a genuinely spontaneous revelation from the Holy Spirit (cp. vs. 29). But glossolalia adds a supernatural aspect that strengthens the divine origin and validity of all of the utterance gifts (including the word of wisdom, word of knowledge, and discerning of spirits).

(B) FIVE WORDS OR TEN THOUSAND

See 1 Co 14:19. In the light of what has gone before, this verse might be expanded to read: "In church I would rather speak five words with my mind, by preaching or prophesying, so that I might instruct others, than to speak ten thousand words in tongues, which only edifies me".

However, let us clearly understand that Paul is not condemning glossolalia nor denying that it has any value. He is stressing only the comparative value and proper use of the vocal gifts in the church. In the context of personal devotion, Paul placed great value on glossolalia -

"I want you all to speak in tongues" (vs. 5)

"I thank God I speak in tongues more than you all" (vs. 18)

"Giving thanks in the spirit is giving thanks well" (vs. 17)

Paul is not setting one gift against another. How could he? Are they not all *gifts of the Holy Spirit*? He is only clarifying the right place, time, and manner in which each gift should be used. There is a time when glossolalia has great value, when the glossolalist is *"edified"*, and *"speaks to God"*, *"uttering mysteries in the spirit"*. Then there is a time when prophecy has great value, when revelation comes to the church, bringing *"upbuilding, encouragement, and consolation."*

The key thought in the passage is the proper edification of the individual, and of the church - especially of the church. Every gift, every manifestation, must submit to this supreme test: **does it edify the church?** Those who speak in tongues edify themselves, and that is splendid for them in their personal devotions; but it brings no benefit to the church, unless the glossolalia is followed by the gift of interpretation. However, someone who prophesies, speaks directly in a language known to all, and thus is eminently useful to the whole church.

Nonetheless, while Paul undoubtedly valued his personal gift of tongues, he does not hesitate to condemn the Corinthian's childish fascination with glossolalia. He urged them to realise that a church meeting in which glossolalia predominated, or in which its exercise was not properly regulated, was nothing less than pagan insanity (vs. 6-11,20,23).

For that reason he uses some strong expressions when he describes a form of worship in which the whole church does little more than shout away in tongues. He calls it a jangling cacophony of discordant instruments, saying that it was like a tuneless bugle, which leaves the soldiers confused. Their worship was an unintelligent chorusing into thin air, like the ravings of insanity *("mainomai"* = to rave"). They were behaving like barbarians *("barbaros"* = a foreigner).

For the Corinthians, the latter word was particularly hurtful. While it could mean just a foreigner, its basic meaning was someone ignorant of the Greek language and culture, a rough and brutal savage, a person whose speech and ways were crude and barbaric. When applied to a Greek it was one of the worst insults that could be offered. The Corinthians, so proud of the excitement, the "spiritual" and highly emotional character of their glossolalia-filled church, must have been staggered to hear Paul linking *"barbaros"* with their worship!

Charismata occupy an important place in Christian worship, and they must be retained in the church. But their use must always be carefully regulated. In particular, charismatic gifts must yield precedence to ministry gifts; and especially, glossolalia must yield to intelligible utterance.

CONCLUSION

Having shown the relative value of the three gifts of utterance, Paul draws a pungent conclusion -

> *"Since you are eager for manifestations of the Spirit, strive to excel in building up the church" (vs. 12).*

This can mean two things -

First: they should, in the exercise of any spiritual gift, strive to use it in its highest form and to the limit of their ability. Then the church will receive the greatest possible edification. Similarly, in Ro 12:6-7 Paul urges them to stir up their utmost faith when they use a spiritual gift. Therefore they should wait continually upon the Lord for the enlarging of that gift, so that its effectiveness might be increased.

Second: they should always seek those gifts that at any given time will most edify the church. In this case the verse would read: "Since you are eager for manifestations of the Spirit, strive for those that will be the very best for building up the church".

In either case there are two criteria that must always be observed:

- ♦ use only those charismata, and use them in a way, that will best edify the church; and
- ♦ seek only those charismata that best suit your place in the body of Christ.

By following those rules, and striving to fulfil the grace and faith you have received from Christ, you will be well equipped to serve the church in the power of the Holy Spirit.

Chapter Nine

ZEAL TO EXCEL!

If *love* is the mark of an individual Christian (Jn 13:35), then **"prophecy"** is the mark of the Spirit-filled church (Ac 2:17-18). As surely as true believers, following the example of Christ, may be known by their demonstration of divine love, so a true church, following the example of the apostles, may be known by the presence of prophecy. What is this *"prophecy"?* The word is used to describe a wide range of inspired speech, sometimes involving a prediction of the future, but more commonly addressed to an immediate situation. Paul declares that its usual purpose in the church is to convey from the heart of God a direct word of *"upbuilding, encouragement, consolation, exhortation, revelation, instruction"* (1 Co 14:3-6). It is addressed to the church, and is a sign to it of the presence of God and of his participation in their worship (vs. 32). Not everyone in the church can possess or use the gift of prophecy (12:29); but the gift should be widely enough bestowed in the congregation for *"two or three"* prophets to speak in a given meeting, and for their words to be judged by other prophets (14:29). In Corinth they were numerous enough for Paul to say, *"you may all prophecy one by one"* (vs. 31).

Because he himself placed high value upon the gift of prophecy, Paul commanded the early Christians to be *"eager to prophesy",* and in their use of the gift to *"strive always for excellence"* (vs. 39, 12).

Prophecy is also a key to spontaneous growth; for Paul pre-supposes that *"unbelievers and outsiders"* will be attracted to a *"prophesying"* church, where they will be brought under irresistible conviction, and then presumably added to the congregation (vs. 24-25).

However, the very power of this gift makes it a special target of Satan; therefore special care must be taken in its use -

(A) A VOLITIONAL GIFT

Neither prophecy nor any other charismatic gift should depend upon mere whim-

> *"You know how when you were pagans you were governed by impulse, doing whatever you were moved to do, as you chased after dumb idols" (12:1-2).*

Paul declares that loss of personal volition is a hallmark of paganism, which means that involuntary behaviour should have no place in Christian practice. Pagans, he says, are prone to surrender to religious and emotional impulse; they do whatever they are "moved" by the god to do; they go wherever they are "moved" to go; they are driven by impulse.

Do you not find it sad to see Christians craving such experiences, as if they represent the quintessence of spiritual maturity and piety? Why do people feel that the pinnacle of happiness is to "lose" oneself in the Lord, to be reduced to some kind of spiritual catalepsy, to a state of automatism? Are we mere puppets dancing at the end of a celestial string? Yet there are Christians who yearn to be prostrated by the Spirit, [a]slain by the Lord, possessed by God, fall into a trance, drained of all self-awareness, and the like. Then there are others who do things because they are "led" to do them, who dare not resist any spiritual impulse, for each prompting reaches them like the voice of God, which must be instantly obeyed. A lifestyle like that reeks more of paganism than it reflects a truly Christian spirituality.

---

[a] See again the Addendum on Religious Prostration that follows Chapter One above

I do not mean that all spontaneous experiences are necessarily wrong or evil; on the contrary, they may be powerful, pleasant, enriching. But you should recognise that such happenings are not inevitably a work of the Holy Spirit, especially if they require a loss of volition. Does not scripture say that one of the finest marks of the presence of the Holy Spirit in a person's life is *"self-control"?* (Ga 22-23). Therefore Paul insists that we must take personal responsibility for what is happening in our own spirits (1 Co 14:32). No one can ever say with truth, "The Lord *made* me do it!"

(B) A CONTROLLED GIFT

Paul's language makes it clear that prophecy is a direct act of the *human* spirit, and only indirectly an act of the *Holy* Spirit (cp. again 1 Co 14:14, *"my spirit prays ... "*).   At once many problems are solved. which arise from the idea that prophecy comes only from the Lord. If the Spirit is involved in prophetic utterances only *indirectly*, then we can understand how prophecies can sometimes be wrong, and why they must be *"judged"* by the church (14:29). It also explains why true prophecies can sometimes be given, even when they are not inspired by the Holy Spirit. Indeed, scripture itself shows that a prophetic gift can function with or without the presence or power of the Holy Spirit - see 1 Co 12:1; 13:2; De 13:1-3. Hence we can observe

(1) FIVE POSSIBLE LEVELS OF PROPHECY

(a) That Which Is Merely Concocted

I once had to deal with a man who gave a prophetic message in church around the theme of the return of Christ. Unfortunately for him, just the night before I had read the same book on the Second Advent that he had obviously read. He wanted to share with the congregation the ideas that were in the book, knew that he would not be able to do so across the pulpit, so he chose to promulgate them under the guise of prophecy.   He was mightily surprised and embarrassed when I confronted him with his deception and placed him under discipline for misusing the gift of God.

Then there are those who by nature are false prophets, of whom you should be aware, and against whom you should be armed -

> *"Her prophets cover up all her blemishes, by delivering a false vision and speaking a false oracle. Even though God has not spoken, yet still they say, 'This is the word of the Lord!'" (Ez 22:28).*

(b) That Which Is Demon-Inspired

Prophetic powers are often attributed to demons in scripture, with the proviso that *"Satan is a liar from the beginning"* (Jn 8:44), therefore he can never wholly tell the truth. Every satanic oracle has some falsehood, the liar cannot avoid corruption, so that only the unwary are deceived.

> *"An evil spirit came and stood before the Lord and said, 'I will be a lying spirit in the mouth of all his prophets'" (1 Kg 22:22).*

> *"The demon cried out, 'I know thee who thou art; the Holy One of God'" (Lu 4:34).*

> *"Demons came out of many people, crying out, and saying, 'Thou art Christ the Son of God'" (Lu 4:41).*

> *"The demoniac fell down before Jesus, and cried at the top of his voice, 'What have I to do with you, Jesus? You are the Son of the Most High God! I beseech you, do not torment me!'" (Lu 8:28).*

> *"A girl possessed by a fortune-telling spirit kept on following Paul and Silas and shouting, 'These men*

*serve the Most High God, and they are telling you
the way of salvation," (Ac 16:16-18).*

*"The Antichrist will come doing the works of Satan,
yet supported by miracles, signs, and lying wonders,
which will deceive and destroy those who love
unrighteousness" (2 Th 2:9).*

*"I saw three unclean spirits like frogs come out of
the mouth of the dragon, and out of the mouth of the
beast, and out of the mouth of the false prophet" (Re
16:13).*

(c) That Which Is Sincere, But Wrong

There is a well-known evangelist who on several occasions has
prophesied over Alison and me. On two or three of those occasions
his oracles were astonishingly accurate. He seemed to know more
about our affairs than we knew ourselves! His words found an
accurate fulfilment in the unfolding of events, and we knew beyond
question that God had spoken to us through his voice.

But on the other occasions his prophecies were either so general as
to have no practical meaning, or were downright wrong!

Yet he was the same man, speaking just as sincerely each time, and
with the same grace of God operating in his ministry. How then
could he be so right sometimes and so wrong other times?

Simply because prophecy comes out of the human spirit, and is
subject to an admixture of error that can hardly be avoided. The
prophet can do no more than strive to rid his or her spirit of all clutter
and open the way for the Holy Spirit to speak as clearly as possible;
but in the end no prophet can be absolutely sure that an oracle comes

wholly from God. That is why all prophetic oracles must be judged - that is, assessed for their accuracy and anointing.[a]

(d) That Which Is Apparently True, But Wrong

I know a pastor who brought himself and his church into bankruptcy because he tossed discretion aside and unwisely allowed himself to be controlled by three prophetic oracles. He had pioneered his church, and it had prospered under the hand of God. The time had come when they needed their own building, but land and property were expensive, and he was reluctant to commit the church to crushing debt. Into that scene, on three separate occasions, came three different visiting preachers, none knowing what the others had said. During the course of their ministry each one of those preachers, using a passage from Ezekiel's vision of the ideal temple, spoke an oracle to the church, declaring that God was going to provide for them a splendid building.

Emboldened by this apparent miracle of prophecy the pastor purchased land, hired an architect, and began to collect materials for a fine sanctuary. Builders were hired, and work on the project began. The church soon ran out of money. The Lord did not provide the supernatural finance they were expecting. The pastor had to sell his own home, cash-in his insurances, and put all his remaining assets into rescuing the church from debt. But it was not enough. Eventually the land and other assets of the church were also seized, and they lost everything.

---

[a] The above comments presume a substantial difference between Old Testament prophecy and the gift of prophecy in the church. The genuine prophets of Israel spoke an infallible word from God; but Christians operate at a different level, for a different purpose, and in a different dimension. You will find more comment on this below.

Some months later I arrived in the town to hold meetings in the same church (now gathering in a rented hall). The pastor was still deeply distressed, and gloom lay over his congregation. He asked me what had gone wrong. Without hesitation I told him that he had been foolish to abandon common sense and fiscal prudence merely on the strength of a prophetic oracle. He protested that the three prophecies were all spoken by good men, and were so similar that he had to accept them as coming from God.

Perhaps. Then again, all three men may have unwittingly responded to subtle signals sent to them by the pastor and by his people.

However, let us suppose that the oracles were genuine; that is, they truly expressed the mind of God for the church. Yet something went wrong, either in the way they were expressed, or in the way they were understood, for it is impossible to suppose that the Holy Spirit would instruct any church to plunge irresponsibly into a morass of debt.

A further lesson from the incident, which I shared with the pastor, is that scripture must always take precedence over some message in prophecy. In his case, the numerous biblical warnings against incurring costs you cannot meet (e.g. Lu 9:28-30) should have been more than enough to hold him back from precipitous response to those three oracles. Never heed any prophecy that speaks against or undermines the plain teaching of scripture. A prophetic oracle may seem to be true, yet may still be wrong.

(e) That Which Is Truly Wrought By The Spirit

Despite the mistakes that can cloud even the most sincere and most anointed prophecies, there remain those times when an oracle comes with all the majesty of heaven. We dare not allow human frailty to lead us to despise prophecy. Paul's advice is obvious and practical -

> *"Never do anything to quench the Spirit's flame.*
> *Never treat prophecies with contempt. Rather, put*

everything to the test, and then hold fast to those things that are good" (1 Th 5:19-20).

(2) WE ARE NOT AUTOMATONS

There is a spurious piety that wants to reduce people to passionless and barren blobs, utterly possessed by the deity, with no mind or will of their own. But men and women cannot be turned into vacuous black-boards, waiting for the scratch of divine chalk. We cannot behave like a camera or a phonograph, faithfully repeating in minute detail whatever is recorded in our spirits. We are bound to interpret what we see, hear, feel, or sense.

Thus you can take a group of artists out into the country to paint a tree, and though they all see the same tree how different their representations of it will be! In just the same way the Holy Spirit plants his word in our spirits, but then leaves each prophet to express it in his or her own way. Think about the four gospels, how differently they each portray Christ!

You should realise also that the human spirit has an ability to generate spiritual activity on its own account, with or without either demonic or divine input. Indeed, some people are highly gifted spiritually (just as others are musically, artistically, and so on), and so can generate remarkable spiritual phenomena. Yet we all have some capacity to perform spiritually, just as we can all draw at least simple shapes, or hum a tune, or mould a piece of clay into some recognisable shape.

So each human spirit is capable of unaided spiritual action. Few people are so spiritually incompetent that they cannot work *anything* in the spiritual dimension. This capacity of the human spirit to act unilaterally is the reason why Paul tells the prophets to take control over their spirits. An untamed, undisciplined spirit is an open door to disaster. Let everyone, then, who speaks in the name of the Lord, do so only under divine inspiration and according to divine order. Which leads us to -

(3) FOUR NECESSARY RULES

Paul's warning to the Thessalonians not to despise prophecy suggests that the difficulty of keeping prophecy pure had already caused an anti-charismatic party to arise in the early church. The same pressures are around us today. But we dare not lose our charismatic identity! So the following rules become imperative -

(a) Disciplined By The Church

Each prophet must remain under the authority of the church, answerable to the leadership of the local church where he or she ministers. Any prophet moving outside the orbit of the church, refusing to accept oversight, should be rejected.

(b) Over-Ruled By Freedom

You must not surrender your liberty to any prophet. You are God's own child, you have personal access to the mind of Christ (1 Co 2:16), you can yourself gain the wisdom of God for your life (Ja 1:5-7). So beware of giving too much authority over your actions to any prophecy. Mark how Paul, though he no doubt respected Agabus and accepted the truth of his prediction, still insisted upon going to Jerusalem (Ac 21:10-14). He would not allow any prophet to usurp his God-given freedom in Christ to decide for himself what action he should take.

(c) Strive To Excel

Prophets should strive to "excel" (Ro 12:6; 1 Co 14:12), they dare not rest on their laurels. Here is another indication that prophecy in the church is as much a work of the human spirit as it is of the Holy Spirit. If prophecy came entirely from heaven, so that the prophet was little more than a mechanical mouthpiece, there would be no need to *"wait upon the gift"*, to develop it in richness and maturity. So people who are called by God to serve as prophets in the church must devote much prayer, meditation, and zeal to their gift. They ought to be striving to grasp an ever-fuller measure of grace and faith, so that their oracles may grow in unction and revelation.

(d) Subject To Judgment

All prophecy must be subject to judgment (vs. 29); but note -

(i) Sometimes false prophecies may also be true (De 13:1-5); so the spiritual content of the prophecy and its spiritual effect are more important than the actual words spoken (cp. 1 Kg 22; Je 28; Mt 7:15-23; 1 Jn 4:1).

(ii) Sometimes a genuine prophecy, whether of blessing (Mi 3:9-12), or of judgment (Je 26:16-19), may be unfulfilled because certain conditions (whether stated or implied) are attached to it.

(iii) Some prophecies involve a lesser and a greater fulfilment. For example, note how many Messianic prophecies were first fulfilled in Israel, or in the Psalmist, and only later in Christ. Likewise, many prophecies about Israel's return from exile had only a partial fulfilment in history and await a greater denouement in days to come.

(iv) Prophecy can be misunderstood; e.g. was it Paul or his companions who misunderstood the Spirit's intent? (Ac 20:22-25, 37-38; 21:4, 9-14).

(v) Prophecy can have an unexpected fulfilment. So there are several Messianic prophecies that can be seen only in hindsight to apply to Christ. Many OT prophecies dealing with Israel find their NT fulfilment in the church - something that no one could have predicted ahead of time.

(vi) Prophecy can be fulfilled in principle, but not in particular. Thus many OT prophecies concerning Israel and the nations were fulfilled in their broad thrust, but not in their specific detail.

(vii) Remember always that even the best of prophets speak only *"in part ... (and) see through a dark glass".*

CONCLUSION

Continual prophecy is the glory of the church. It is the special sign of the new era of the Spirit. Let us then never quench nor grieve the Spirit. Let us rather fulfil Ro 12:11, never flagging in zeal, always aglow in the Spirit, serving the Lord in the full power of Pentecost until the day Jesus comes!

Chapter Ten

GRACE AND DIGNITY

From Paul's description it seems that the worship of the people at Corinth was confused and disorderly (1 Co 14:26-33). For that kind of practice the apostle had only scorn. He refused to condone worship that was based upon impulse and so-called "divine leading". He taught that worship should be controlled, and that it is the responsibility of the church itself to see that all things are done *"decently and in order"* (vs. 40).

"Decently" means in a "well-formed" manner, with grace and beauty, becomingly and with discipline.

"In order" means "arranged in an orderly manner", with proper balance, and with each part of the service following the other in proper succession.

Some Pentecostal churches (despite Paul) still have a tendency to flatter themselves on the "freedom" (read "ungraceful" and "disorderly") of their style of worship. With high disdain they despise churches that follow a set liturgy, and boast that no one ever knows what is going to happen next in *their* services. Fortunately most of the Pentecostal movement has long since escaped from such libertarian nonsense, and has regulated itself in conformity with Paul's instructions.

The fact is, only by the wise use of order can people properly prepare themselves for each new act of worship. If worship is to be *intelligent* as well as *spiritual* (cp. vs. 14-16; Jn.4:24) then it must be structured to appeal to the mind as well as to the soul. True worship cannot be a thing of momentary whim or subjective fancies, nor merely a thing of emotional response.

However, it is equally against scripture to build a style of worship so rigidly structured, so filled with liturgical activity, that the people are allowed no freedom for spontaneous expression, or for an occurrence of spiritual gifts. True Pentecostal worship will have enough order to maintain grace, beauty, dignity, and an intelligent and responsible involvement of the people; but also enough freedom to allow for immediate guidance and direct intervention by the Holy Spirit.

Against that background, let us explore

(I) THE PURPOSE OF THE CHARISMATA

The glory of the charismata (and especially of the three vocal gifts) does not rest in the fact that they *exist*, but that they achieve their *purpose* in the church -

(A) THEIR PARTICULAR PURPOSE

See 1 Co 14:3,5; from which we can conclude that no genuine prophecy or interpretation of tongues will be:

derisive- for they should *strengthen* the people
critical- for they should *encourage* the people
negative-for they should *comfort* the people
destructive-for they should *edify* the people
directive-for they should *instruct* the people.

The church must not hesitate to *"judge"* each oracle by such criteria, and to bring under discipline those prophets who refuse to submit to these rules (vs. 29; and see also below)

(B) THEIR GENERAL PURPOSE

Arising from the above, we can say that the charismata are given

- ♦ to equip the church to be the body of Christ; that is, to enable it to do what Jesus himself would do if he were here in the flesh; and
- ♦ to draw us into a closer relationship with Christ (12:3).

Faced with such a lofty aim, we must learn the lessons of -

(1) CONTROL

Mature spiritual understanding will accept that the charismata can and must be controlled (1 Co 14:20,32, 26-38). Plainly we are told that *"the spirits of prophets are subject to prophets".* So any person who thinks himself or herself to be a prophet, or spiritual, will accept the limitations on the exercise of these gifts set down by Paul.

(2) MYSTERY

Many people do not understand how these supernatural gifts can be subject to human control. How can the works of the Holy Spirit be open to wrongful use by sinful men and women? It is indeed a great mystery. The manner in which the Lord has made these priceless endowments so freely available to the church, and subject to human control, is truly amazing. But our task is not to reason how or why. We should simply accept the gifts of God and humbly yield to his own commands concerning their use.

However, we should understand that the rules laid down by the apostle do not limit the Holy Spirit (which would be absurd), but only the *human* spirit (vs. 14-16). The fact that these sacred gifts are resident in us places upon us an awesome responsibility to use them well.

(II) THE LIMITS OF THE CHARISMATA

(A) CONCERNING TONGUES AND INTERPRETATION

The rules are explicit and clear:

- ♦ only two or at most three are to give a prophetic utterance in tongues in any one meeting
- ♦ those who do so are to speak *"each in turn"*, that is, one at a time, and at the properly appointed time in the service

♦ if no *"interpreter"* is present, the glossolalists must *"keep silence in church"*; however, that is not an absolute prohibition, for if the church service has come to a time of praise and worship, the glossolalists may join with the whole congregation in *"speaking to God"*

♦ such *"speaking to God"* may be *"with the spirit"* (in glossolalia) or *"with the mind"* (in the vernacular; cp. vs. 15, 2).

(B) CONCERNING INTERPRETATION

(1) Paul uses the noun *"diermeneutes"* = "an interpreter" (vs. 28), which suggests a specially recognised ministry. For example, he could have said, *"if there is no one with the gift of interpretation"*; but his use of the word *"interpreter"* carries the sense of a more or less permanent responsibility. Anybody might give a message in tongues (vs. 5), but only *"interpreters"* could exercise the gift of interpretation. That is probably because a certain natural fluency is needed before one can render into common speech an interpretation equal in power and content to a richly anointed message in tongues.

(2) The rule is: *"let one interpret"* (vs. 27). Three views are common here:

♦ that two or three glossolalists should speak, and then a single interpretation be given for them all; or

♦ that the same person in any particular meeting should interpret each glossolalic utterance; or

♦ that only one interpretation is to be given for each glossolalic utterance, although it may be a different interpreter in each case.

I prefer the third view.

(3) Experience has shown that interpreters should not concentrate on the words that are being spoken in tongues. Rather they should wait upon the Lord and open their minds to the revelation of the

Spirit. *"Interpretation"* ("exposition") does not require a word-for-word "translation", but rather an unfolding of the spiritual *meaning* of the utterance in tongues. An interpretation may therefore be approximately the same length as the utterance with which it is associated, or it may be much shorter or longer - whatever is required to bring the message of the Spirit to the church.

(C) CONCERNING PROPHECY

(1) The word *"prophets"* in verses 29 & 32 must be given the general sense of those who use the *spiritual gift* (charisma) of prophecy. It probably should not be taken to refer to the distinct *ministry gift* of a prophet (Ep 4:11). Although there is no sharp distinction between them in the NT, it seems fair to say that a *prophet* is one of the ministry-gifts that operates (like an evangelist) across many churches, while the gift of *prophecy* is a local church function.

(2) Two or three people may exercise the gift of prophecy in a given meeting, and others have the right to judge whether or not each prophecy is truly anointed by the Holy Spirit. The gift of prophecy in the church differs markedly from the inspired prophetic utterances of the prophets of Israel. They spoke the direct word of the Lord, and they spoke in the first person (e.g. Is 27:2-4; Je 51:24-25; Ez 2213-16; etc). The nearest equivalent in the church to the former prophets, are the inspired writings we call the New Testament. The gift of prophecy set in the church serves the more limited purpose of *"edifying"* the body. Its inspiration is momentary, its purpose is temporary. It is not infallible. It is not "the word of the Lord" in the sense that scripture is; it may not be used to command the church; it cannot convey new doctrine.

If it were expected that the gift of prophecy should be infallible, or that we should yield to it the same authority as the prophets or old claimed for their pronouncements, Paul could not have commanded *"let two or three prophets speak, <u>and let the others weigh what is said</u>"* (vs. 29).

Excursus: The Use of the First Person

Because the gift issues primarily out of the *human* spirit, and because it must be *"judged"*, it seems better to avoid the use of the first person. If someone delivers a prophecy as if God himself were speaking, then he or she arrogates an authority to their utterance that it simply does not have. Further, such a claim must preclude the church from *"judging"* the prophecy. After all, how can I presume to tell God that he is mistaken? So all prophecies, interpretations of tongues, words of knowledge, etc, should be spoken in a way that leaves the hearers free to assess for themselves whether or not these revelations come from God.

For the same reasons, it seems advisable to avoid prefacing or concluding the utterance with such phrases as "thus says the Lord", or, "thus says the Spirit" - unless, of course, the claim is related to a direct quotation of scripture. (These restrictions apply also to the gift of interpretation.)[a]

(3) The statement *"you may all prophecy one by one"* (vs. 31) does not contradict the earlier *"let two or three prophets speak"*. In a given service, there should be only two or three utterances in prophecy; but the prophets should make themselves aware of the

---

[a] I recall an embarrassing evening in a Christian coffee shop when an attractive young woman stood up, her eyes closed, her arms outstretched, and began to prophecy in the first person: "I love you with all my heart. You are my dearly beloved. Run into my arms and find comfort. My hand stretches out to you in love. Why do you linger? Come now! Come quickly! I am waiting to give you all of my love…etc" I hardly dare imagine what the "unbelievers and outsiders" made of that! It was one occasion when much glossolalia probably would have been less offensive than prophecy! Yet there would have been no problem at all if she had simply used the third person "The Lord loves you…etc"

inspiration being received by their fellow prophets, and defer to one another, so that all in turn have an opportunity to exercise their gift (vs. 30). (The word *"all"* probably refers to *"all the prophets"* rather than *to "all the members of the congregation".*)

Excursus: Women Prophesying (vs. 34,35)

No one really knows what Paul meant by his rule about women keeping silence in the church, nor why he gave it. But before jumping to the conclusion that no woman may rightly prophecy in the church, note that

- ◆ his prohibition is only against married women asking questions; and
- ◆ he himself allowed women to prophesy (11:5), which inevitably had to be done in the church, subject to "judgment", and for the "edifying" of the church (and cp. also Philip's four daughters who were *"prophetesses"*, Ac 21:8-9).

(D) THE NEED FOR "JUDGMENT"

Paul commands *"the others* (the church, or the prophets) *to weigh what is said"* in a prophetic utterance, or in an interpretation of tongues (1 Co 14:29). The word *"weigh"* is "diakrino" = *"to weigh up",* "to discriminate between," to use proper "discernment". Each prophetic oracle must be *"weighed"* -

(1) as to whether it was merely an emotional outburst, or a genuine revelation of the Holy Spirit, given under the control of a sanctified will, spoken with wisdom, and in accordance with scripture.

It is futile for anyone who has wrongfully used one of the utterance gifts to say, "I could not stop myself speaking; I was compelled by the Lord!" The scripture is emphatic: *"the spirits of prophets are subject to prophets.*

(2) as to whether it has fulfilled its divinely given purpose in the church.

The gifts of utterance are set in the church to *bring "upbuilding, encouragement, consolation, edification, learning"*; therefore every true exercise of these gifts will achieve one or more of those goals. The glory, power, and value of the charismata in the church is not the mere fact that they are occurring, *but that they are achieving their intended purpose.* Without that, they are worthless.

(E) SOME PRACTICAL CONCLUSIONS

(1) If the gifts are functioning properly, then the exercise of one gift will not contradict or countermand another. For example, a prophecy on the theme of sorrow for sin would hardly be followed by an interpretation on the theme of praise. The Holy Spirit does not war against himself in the church.

(2) A genuine gift (which is given to "edify") will not be vindictive, invidious, harsh, discourteous, destructive (cp. 1 Pe 3:8; Ja 3:17-18).

(3) A genuine gift will glorify Christ, lift the worship and praise of the people, and be in harmony with the ministry gifts of Christ in the church. For example, a sermon on the need for prayer would hardly be followed by a prophecy cancelling that need.

(4) If an utterance cannot be clearly heard by the entire congregation, then it has failed in its purpose to edify the church, and must be ruled out of order. Those with soft voices should find other ways to serve God and the church.

(5) Those who are visiting a church must submit their gifts to the customs and order prevailing in that church. In fact, I would generally consider it imprudent for any person to exercise any of the charismata in a church until after he or she became familiar with the customary pattern followed by that congregation.

(6) If a message is poorly delivered, or expressed in such a way as to leave its meaning doubtful, then it has failed to edify the church, and the person so using the gifts must be corrected. On this point, notice -

(a) People should be encouraged to use modern English when delivering a prophetic message to the church. There is no virtue in using the English of King James, and few people use it correctly anyway. In fact it would probably be good to rid the church of all such archaic language. The early church was content to use the everyday language of the people in all parts of its worship, and there is no good reason why we should not do the same.

(b) While we should always strive for excellence in the use of the charismata, scope must be given for people to develop their gift. Paul sets a good example here. There appears to have been an anti-charismata faction in the church at Corinth, at Thessalonica, and possibly in other churches also (1 Co 14:37-39; 1 Th 5:19-21). The Corinthian faction seemingly wanted to banish all charismatic utterances. The Thessalonian faction may not have been so bold, but it was at least guilty *of "quenching the Spirit"* by *"despising"* prophecy. Both factions were rebuked by Paul. But what could have caused this dislike of prophetic oracles? The answer apparently lies in the poor quality of many such utterances. Not all the prophets (whether then or now) were able to reach a high level of inspiration, or to maintain it constantly. Perhaps the edification gained by the church from prophecies was often minimal. Some felt that the best solution was to ban such utterances altogether, but not Paul -

(i) He insisted that charismata should be encouraged (*"desire the spiritual gifts"*), and that they were neither to be forbidden nor despised.

(ii) The churches should recognise the different measure of grace, faith, spiritual unction, that the various prophets had received from God (Ro 12:1-6). Those who possess charismatic gifts should be encouraged to wait on God for the continual

enlargement of the gift; but in the meantime, they should be permitted to exercise their gift to the best of their ability.

(iii) Each prophetic utterance should be received charitably and given due respect. The church has a mandate to *"weigh"* each utterance, to *"test everything"*, and out of each prophecy to *"hold fast what is good"* and to discard the remainder. But it must not throw out the tablecloth with the crumbs, nor the wheat with the chaff. Prophecy must not be rejected simply because some oracles fail to display exalted inspiration. The church must use discrimination in how far it accepts a given utterance as divinely inspired; but that discrimination must not extend to the banning of prophecy.

(c) Each church should guard against thinking that its particular manner of exercising the vocal gifts is divinely ordained. Only two rules concerning the exercise of these gifts are given in scripture:

- that no more than two or three prophets and/or glossolalists are to speak in a given service; and
- that the exercise of each gift must edify the church.

All other details are unspecified, and must arise from the order and custom followed by each church:

- some churches will use modern idiom, while others prefer the language of the King James Bible
- some churches will expect prophets to speak with closed eyes; others will tell them to keep their eyes open
- some churches will expect the prophet to speak with outward signs of "unction" - rapidly, forcefully, with emotion; while others will prefer natural and calm speech
- some churches will want these gifts to be a part of every meeting; others will restrict their use to certain specified meetings; etc.

(7) Once the prescribed limit of two or three utterances in prophecy, and/or in tongues and interpretation, has been reached, no amount of "anointing" or "leading" should be taken as a warrant to

break the rule of scripture. The person who feels impelled to speak, who senses the pent-up power of the Holy Spirit, should express himself (or herself) in prayer, praise, or in any other way that is acceptable to the church. Paul's word is emphatic, relentless: *"the spirits of prophets are subject to prophets"*.

(8) Paul writes: *"If a new revelation comes to another sitting by, let the first be silent"* (1 Co 14:30). There are three possible ways to apply that instruction -

(a) Paul allows a second prophet to stand up and interrupt the first, whereupon the first must stop speaking and sit down. At first sight, that is what Paul appears to be saying; yet it seems contrary to the spirit of the passage, which is concerned with the smooth and orderly conduct of the meeting. Such an abrupt interruption hardly seems consistent with *"let all things be done decently and in order"*.

(b) A second view would read the verse this way: *"If a new revelation comes to another sitting by, let (the second speaker wait until) the first (is) silent."* That is more paraphrase than translation, and it stretches the Greek uncomfortably. But it does have the support of a couple of modern translations. It also has the added advantage of being consistent with the general theme of Paul's discussion, which, once again, is proper order in the church.

(c) A third suggestion, put forward by Leon Morris, is that

"certain prophets would normally be selected to speak, but the possibility might always arise of a direct revelation being given to another sitting by. The designated speaker should in this case give way".

The suggestion is attractive; but it implies a regimentation of the prophets that seems to be incompatible with the generally spontaneous nature of the charismata.

Whatever interpretation is followed, the main sense is plain: Paul is commanding the prophets to defer to each other graciously, so that they may all have opportunity to exercise their gift while maintaining balance and beauty in the church meetings. There should be no disorder, no striving for precedence, but a generous willingness to defer to each other in love.

(F) EDIFY THE CHURCH

Let me stress this point again: prophetic gifts are not for private use or benefit. They are set in *the church* for the purpose of edifying *the church*. So their use should not be encouraged in a merely private or family setting, nor where a handful of Christians have gathered for fellowship or prayer. Using the charismata in such settings must be discouraged by those who have oversight in the church. Experience has shown that where prophetic gifts are permitted to flourish outside of the responsible oversight of the church, or in a private way, they nearly always lapse into disorder, or false revelation, or radical fanaticism.

Many people have brought spiritual ruin upon themselves and others because they insisted on a private use of the charismata and refused to bring them under the control and discipline of the church.

Some would argue that where "two or three" Christians are gathered in the name of the Lord, there you have a church; thus they feel free to exercise spiritual gifts and to fulfil all the functions of a church. I will agree, of course that every church has its nucleus in Christian people gathering in the name of Jesus; but that is insufficient as a definition of a church. In the full biblical sense of the term a church exists only when several other factors are present. What are they?

- Louise Berkhof: the true preaching of the Word of God.
               the right administration of a sacrament.
               the faithful exercise of discipline.

- A. H. Strong: formal organisation into a recognised body.
united worship, prayer, and instruction.
oversight by pastors and deacons.
the exercise of discipline.
observance of baptism.
observance of the Lord's Supper.

- C. F. Hunter: united public worship at stated times,
the sacrament of baptism.
the sacrament of the Lord's Supper.
proclamation of the Word of God.
formal organisation.
under responsible oversight.
the presence of an ordained ministry.

- William Pope: the sacrament of baptism.
the sacrament of the Lord's Supper.
public worship.
preaching of the Word of God.
fellowship, building Christian character

- William Smith: stated and public worship.
preaching the Word, and prayer.
sacraments of baptism and the eucharist.
the pastoral office and the diaconate.

- Anglican Church "a congregation of faithful men in the which
(Art. XIX): the pure word of God is preached, and the
sacraments be duly ministered according to
Christ's ordinance in all those things that of
necessity are requisite to the same."

Examples could be multiplied; but there seems to be a general
agreement among commentators as to the things that are necessary

before a group of people can call themselves a local church. My own list would include at least -

- a formal union as a worshipping body
- regular and public worship
- the preaching of the Word of God
- the sacraments of baptism and communion
- training in Christian character
- a recognised pastoral office
- a functioning oversight (diaconate, or eldership)
- the exercise of church discipline.

Spiritual gifts are restricted by the rule of scripture to operation within the framework of such a church, or under its supervision and responsible judgment. This is especially true of the voice gifts, which are specifically related to the gathered company of worshipping believers.

Chapter Eleven

GLORIES OF GLOSSOLALIA

In this chapter I plan to compile a list, in scriptural order, of the most significant references to glossolalia, and to use them as a foundation upon which to build a study of the nature of glossolalia, and of its use and value in Christian devotional life.

(A) MARK 16:17,30

Whether or not this passage was an original part of Mark's gospel, it still demonstrates the belief of the early church that one of the major functions of glossolalia (as of all the more spectacular charismata) was *"confirmation of the gospel by the signs that followed it"*. This confirmatory character of glossolalia is a theme that is often stated or implied in scripture. This is one of its chief values to the Spirit-filled believer. Glossolalia speaks to the believer in two ways:

- ♦ *subjectively*, by its effects on his or her personal life; and
- ♦ *objectively*, as a phenomenon that can be tangibly observed, which began at a definite point in his life, and which stands as a fulfilment of scripture.

It also carries a witness of the resurrection and ascension of Christ, and as a sign of the indwelling Spirit (Ac 2:32-33).

The early church was proud of its *"signs following"* gospel, and the apostles often referred to the supernatural witness that attended their ministry - Ac 2:22,43; etc; Ro 15:18-19; 1 Co 2:4; 2 Co 12:12; 1 Th 1:5; He 2:4; etc. Our need of this witness is no less than theirs.

(B) JOHN 7:37-39

I have suggested elsewhere that the clause, *"out of his heart shall flow rivers of living water"* is probably a picturesque way of describing what Paul calls *"praying in the spirit"* (that is, with glossolalia). If that is so, then glossolalia may be described as a river unleashed by the Holy Spirit to satisfy deep spiritual thirst. Jesus said that this blessing was promised in scripture. No such specific prophecy exists in the Old Testament, so the Lord probably meant only that this general promise lay in all the scriptures. But he may also have had in mind such places as Is 35:1-6 (*"then shall ... the tongue of the dumb sing for joy. For waters shall break forth in the wilderness, and streams in the desert"*). Or perhaps Ez 47:1 ff., which describes a stream of living water flowing out from the inner part of the temple (a picture of the human spirit?), bringing life and healing to every place it touched. Those who have experienced glossolalia find in both analogies an apt description of what the gift of tongues has meant to them.

(C) ACTS 2:4

The events of the Day of Pentecost, and later similar happenings in Acts, show that glossolalia is a definitive sign of Holy Spirit baptism. Those who speak in tongues find an important value in the constant proof glossolalia gives of the Spirit's empowerment. It is hard to think of a more effective sign, especially in view of the importance of the human tongue in worship and prayer. Our capacity for speech, and especially to speak creatively, is one of the chief marks that we are made in the *"image and likeness of God"*. After all, the first thing the Bible tells us about God is that he spoke: *"God said ... "* There is indeed some mysterious power in the human voice, which is not shared by any other created being, not even the angels (cp. Pr 12:14; 18:20-21, 4; Mk.7:29; 11:23; Ro 10:9-10; Nu 20:8; and cp. Ro 4:17-21). To use the vivid phrase of the psalmist, my voice is *"my glory"* - see 16:9; 30:12; 57:8; 108:1; etc. In those places the Hebrew word (*"kabod"*) is frequently translated as "soul"; but that is pedestrian.

"Kabod" means "splendour"; and the reference is more probably to the human voice as the instrument of praise that lifts us into the heavenlies. God, when imparting to me the gift that reveals *his* glory, which is his Spirit, establishes that gift through the sign that reveals *my* glory, which is my voice (especially when it speaks supernatural praise).

(D) ROMANS 8:15-16

> *"When we cry, 'Abba! Father!' it is the Spirit himself bearing witness with our spirit that we are children of God" (also Ga 4:6).*

Two words used there by Paul show that he is referring to glossolalia-

(1) *"Krazo"* = "to cry". This is an onomatopoeic word, echoing the hoarse call of a raven. It was used by the Greeks to describe a raven's cry, and then, by analogy, to describe a human scream or inarticulate shout. It is a cry made with deep emotion and great excitement. It was often used, as here, to describe an impulsive cry wrought out of powerful spiritual feeling.

(2) *"Abba"* = an Aramaic diminutive for "Father" - akin to "Daddy!" It was the familiar term used by children in the home to address their father. It was also a proper noun, whose use was forbidden to slaves, for it belonged only to the freeborn children of the domestic father.

Paul says that when the Holy Spirit comes upon us, thus proving that we are the children of God, our spirits at once respond by crying aloud, "Abba!" This fervent cry may be in our own language, but it seems more probable that Paul is using *"Abba"* to express the "krazon" of glossolalia. *"Abba"* then stands for the whole range of glossolalic utterance, and it reveals the nature and meaning of that utterance - it is my spirit in joyful recognition crying ***"Daddy!"***

Along with *"Abba"* ("Daddy") Paul linked the formal Greek word for father - *"Pater"*. You will hardly suppose that the early Christians went around crying aloud, *"Abba! Pater!"* So what does Paul mean by this mysterious phrase? He seems to be attempting to summarise the content of two kinds of utterance inspired by the Holy Spirit: **prayer with the spirit, and prayer with the understanding** (1 Co 14:14-15) -

(a) As Spirit-filled Christians we can pray with **understanding**, that is, in our natural language, with an intelligent realisation of our relationship with God. He is in heaven, we are upon earth (Ec 5:1-2); so we approach him reverently and address him with the formal and respectful designation, "Father" *("Pater").*

(b) But as Spirit-filled Christians we can also pray with the **spirit**, that is, in a supernatural language, glossolalia. This form of prayer is comprehended in the exclamation, *"Abba - Daddy!"* We could not presume to speak so familiarly to God in our natural language. But the Spirit himself inspires the spontaneous outpouring of glossolalia; therefore this utterance is aptly characterised by Paul as the love-cry of a child to its adored parent. *"Abba"* is not the word of a rational, formal relationship, but the joy-filled outburst of unreasoning trust and delight.

It is good to *"pray with the mind"* - to address God formally as "Father." But it is also good to *"pray with the spirit"* - and to know that the sentiment and significance of glossolalia is richly summarised in the happy cry, *"ABBA!"*

(E) 1 CORINTHIANS 14:2

(1) Glossolalia is a means of direct communion with God; it provides a way of instant access to the throne of God; it can be exercised in the midst of a host of other mind-distracting activities. Because of those factors, and others like them, it provides a means of keeping the soul in constant fellowship with the Spirit. The main exceptions to that statement occur when:

- ♦ the gift of tongues is used in connection with interpretation to bring a prophetic message to the church; and when

♦ a special miracle occurs to make the tongue intelligible to a listener (as on the day of Pentecost, Ac 2:1-11).

However, the day of Pentecost may not have been a simple manifestation of glossolalia; perhaps the intelligibility of those tongues arose from the superimposing of a special miracle onto ordinary glossolalia.

(2) Paul says that when we speak in tongues *we "utter mysteries in the spirit."* He uses the word *"musterion"*, which has some interesting connections –

(a) W. E. Vine links *"musterion"* with "the mysteries" practised among the ancient Greeks - that is, the religious rites observed by secret societies and imposed upon anyone who desired to join them. People who were initiated into those sacred mysteries became possessors of knowledge hidden from the rest of the world, and they were called "the perfected." Against that familiar background Paul deliberately spoke about certain Christian "mysteries" and about the "perfect" men and women who have access to them (1 Co 2:6-16). In particular he links that "perfection" with Holy Spirit baptism and the charismata (vs. 9-10,12,14.) On the same passage, Irenaeus (130-202 A.D.) commented -

"The apostle says, 'We speak wisdom among the perfect,' and by 'the perfect' he means those who had received the Spirit of God, and who spoke in many tongues by the Holy Spirit, as he himself also spoke. Still today we can hear many brethren in the Church who possess prophetic gifts, and who speak in all sorts of languages through the Spirit. Thus they bring to open day the ... mysteries of God; that is why the apostle calls them spiritual."[a]

So a century after Paul's death the churches were still enjoying glossolalia, and fully appreciated the significance of *"speaking*

---

[a] Against Heresies V.6.1.

mysteries in the spirit." Here is wisdom, here is perfection, here is revelation, here is communion with God that the ungifted cannot know! Here is a joy reserved only for those who have yielded themselves to the Spirit and to his divine gifts!

I hope Paul's indictment cannot be spoken against you, gentle reader: "unspiritual people do not receive the gifts of the Spirit of God, for they are folly to them, and they cannot understand them, because they are spiritually discerned" (1 Co 2:14). Rather, may you be fully initiated into Christ by "receiving the Spirit" (vs. 12), thus becoming one of "the perfect" among whom "wisdom" is spoken (vs. 6), who "understand the gifts bestowed upon us by God" (vs. 12). They "possess the Spirit" (vs. 13), and therefore may "utter mysteries" in other tongues; they thus experience what Paul meant when he wrote, *"for the Spirit searches everything, even the depths of God"* (vs. 10).

(b) *"Musterion"* may also imply that when someone is speaking in tongues, the Holy Spirit is drawing out the deepest secrets of the heart, things perhaps unknown or only dimly perceived, even by the speaker. By this divine form of prayer, the most hidden parts of our lives are being searched and exposed by the Holy Spirit, and presented to God for cleansing and refurbishment.

(c) More simply, glossolalic utterances are *"mysteries"* because the meaning of the tongue is unknown. This is confirmed by comparison with vs. 3 - *"on the other hand, someone who prophesies speaks to the church."* The glossolalist speaks to God, because those mysterious tongues convey meaning only to God; but the prophet, speaking in the vernacular, can address the church.

The clause, *"for those who speak in tongues are not speaking to people but to God",* should prevent any attempt to interpret, or understand, a private use of glossolalia. When spoken to God in personal prayer, praise, worship, glossolalia consists of *"mysteries"* that are not addressed to people and have no need to be understood by them. Interpretation belongs only to the special "gift" of tongues, which should be addressed to the church, for the edification of the church.

Notice the contrast here: the church finds edification by tongues *interpreted*; but the individual finds edification by tongues *without* interpretation, spoken to God as "mysteries."

      (d) However, as well as the sense of *"abba"* outlined above, some indication of the meaning of devotional glossolalia may be gained from Ac 2:11; 10:46; Ep 5:18-19. Those verses link glossolalia with *telling "the wonderful works of God," "magnifying God," "psalms and hymns,"* and *"giving thanks,"* and perhaps show something of how glossolalia reaches the heart of God.

(F) 1 CORINTHIANS 14:4

"Those who speak in tongues edify themselves". In its context, that statement draws a disparaging contrast between the personal gain brought by glossolalia and the collective gain brought by prophecy. In the church, prophecy is the preferred gift. However, isolated from a church setting, if Paul were questioned again about the personal value of glossolalia, he would certainly give the same answer, but with a positive accent: *"glossolalia is good for you!"* (NEB). And he would probably add: *"I want you all to speak in tongues, and I thank God that I speak in tongues more than all of you do"* (vs. 5,18).

The word translated *"edify"* is *"oikodomeo"* = a house builder. It is here used figuratively in the sense of promoting spiritual growth. The way Paul connects the word with both glossolalia and prophecy shows his belief that both gifts are valuable. Speaking in tongues can bring the same benefit to the believer's inner spiritual life as prophecy brings to the whole church. Two basic uses of the word can be seen -

(1) To build up

A number of writers have suggested four ways in which glossolalia can "build up" the believer -

(a) Mentally

Not by an inflow of ideas (for *"the mind is unfruitful"* when a person is praying in the spirit), but rather by a release of mental tension. While the spirit is engaged in speaking in tongues, the mind can be at rest in the joy and love of God; it is washed, refreshed, and strengthened by that pure flow of living water (cp. Jn 7:38; Is 28:11-12; 32:2-4.)

(b) Morally

Is 35:3-6 may be taken as a vivid prophecy of the day when the Spirit was to be outpoured. And the result? The tongue is released to sing for joy, and new strength pours into the Spirit-filled believer's heart and mind.

(c) Physically

The early church coupled glossolalia with the healing power of God (cp. Mk 16:17-18; and see also Is 40:31.)

(d) Spiritually

Speaking in tongues is the one distinctly separate and unique exercise of which the human spirit is capable. Paul describes at least three kinds of personal worship in the spirit -

First: "praying in the spirit" (1 Co 14:15).

When we are beset by weakness; when we do not know how to pray as we ought, or even what we should pray for; when the words of ordinary speech are just not sufficient to express our sighs and yearnings; then the Spirit himself can pray for us with feelings too deep for natural speech (Ro 8:26-27).

When we pray in the vernacular, we should mostly pray for others; but when we ourselves need prayer then it is good to pray in the spirit - for as we do so the Holy Spirit *will "intercede for (us) according to the will of God."* And of course, since the Father knows all hearts, he will know what is the mind of the Spirit. This is a prayer in which there can be no intrusion of our self-will, for it is expressed entirely in words created by the Holy Spirit; it must therefore be totally in harmony with God's will!

I would like to repeat though, that we should usually pray in the spirit only when *"we do not know how to pray as we should."* It would generally be improper to try to pray in tongues about a particular matter, or to try to understand the content of glossolalic prayer. When we know what to pray for, we should pray "with the mind," in our ordinary speech.

Further references to *"praying in the spirit,"* which probably refer to glossolalic prayer, occur in Ph 3:3; Ju 20; and Ep 6:18, where both kinds of prayer are mentioned: *"prayer"* (with the mind), and *"supplication in the spirit"* (with glossolalia).

Second: "singing in the spirit."

This is surely a superb method of thanksgiving and of rejoicing! Paul mentions it again in Ep 5:19; Cl 3:16 (*"spiritual songs"*). Somebody may object that there can be no possible benefit in offering irrational and unintelligible worship to God. However, it is a fallacy to suppose that worship and praise must always comprise intelligent communication with God. See, for example, Psalm 150, where the people are commanded to praise God and the dance, and with all kinds of musical instruments, even with *"loud clashing cymbals!"*

Third: "blessing with the spirit" (1 Co 14:16).

The word is *"eulogeo="* to speak well of ... to celebrate with thanksgiving ... to make happy ... to eulogise." If I can bless God, and bring him pleasure, by worshipping him with glossolalia, then I shall do so as often and as fervently as I can! Some translators suggest that vs. 18 should read, *"I give thanks to God by speaking in tongues more than any of you."* If that is so, it shows Paul's recognition of the vital place glossolalia should have in every believer's personal offering of worship and praise to God.

Returning now to *"oikodomeo";* we have seen that it means "to build up." It also means -

(2) To confirm

This word is used in a variety of ways that relate to the benefits glossolalia can bring to the believer.

(a) *"To add strength"* - as when someone says, "Physical prowess is confirmed by constant exercise." The incredible fortitude, stamina, courage, and labours shown by Paul were attributed by him to the *"grace"* ("charis") God had given him (1 Co 15:10). That grace was certainly linked with the spiritual fullness he spoke about when he said, *"I thank God I speak in tongues more than all of you!"*

(b) *"To settle or establish"* - as when someone says, "I am happy to confirm your appointment." So Paul indicates that glossolalia is a confirmation of our initiation into the *"mysteries"* of the gospel of Christ, a sign that we are among the *"perfect"* (see notes above).

(c) *"To give assurance"* - as when someone says, "My hopes are now fully confirmed." So Paul rejoices that the Spirit poured into our lives, and the "cry" he brings *("krazon"),* gives us complete assurance that we are the children of God, and that our inheritance in Christ is secure (Ro 8:14-18).

(d) *"To ratify an agreement"* - as when someone says, "The manager confirms that the contract has been approved." Paul calls the charismatic infilling of the Spirit *"a seal ... which is the guarantee of our inheritance until we acquire possession of it"* (Ep 1:13). The word *"seal"* is *"sphragizo"* and carries a sense of security and permanency. It was the proof of guaranteed ownership, especially ownership secured by a specific mark or sign - in this case, the presence of the Holy Spirit, attested by glossolalia.

(e) *"To strengthen in purpose"* - as when someone says, "Your words strengthen my resolve to go on." So Jude affirms that "praying in the spirit" will assist believers to be "built up in their most holy faith ... (and to) keep themselves in the love of God (while they) wait for the mercy of our Lord Jesus Christ and for eternal life" (vs. 20-21).

However, this "edifying" ability of glossolalia is not a magic panacea. It will not automatically be communicated to any person who uses the gift. The *manner* in which the gift is used is all-important. It is as though someone says: "I have the gift of tongues. What will I do with it? Will I use it to serve myself, for my own gain and aggrandisement? No! I will use this precious gift for the glory of God; I will channel it exclusively into prayer, or song, or blessing in the spirit."

So we must determine never to speak in tongues carelessly or carnally, nor ever just for the mere sake of speaking in tongues. The act of speaking in tongues, by itself, brings no edification; it may be only any empty repetition of sounds (1 Co 13:1). Glossolalia is useful only when it is used

- ♦ to worship God in prayer, song, or eulogy; or
- ♦ to address the church prophetically.

Even then, its use must be injected with genuine love and sincere faith, or its purpose will fail.

(G) 1 CORINTHIANS 14:21-23

Paul calls glossolalia "a sign for unbelievers", which is a statement based on a quotation from Is 28:11-12. First, look at this prophecy in its local setting -

(1) The Tongue of the Assyrians (Is 28:7-13)

Isaiah condemned the false priests of Israel for their drunkenness and debauchery, and he may also have been metaphorically castigating their false doctrines (vs. 7-8). The priests and their followers replied with sarcastic scorn, claiming that Isaiah insulted them with his incessant repetitions of the laws of God. He was treating them, they complained, like infants (vs. 9-10). So the prophet warned them. If they would not listen to his so-called prattling tongue, then God would speak to them through another stammering voice - the foreign tongue of the Assyrians, who were even then pressing against the northern frontiers of Israel (vs. 11). However, they refused to acknowledge the clear signs of impending destruction, and they scornfully rejected Isaiah's pleadings - *"they refused to hear"* (12b). So Isaiah declared that God would harden their hearts; then the word of the Lord would indeed seem foolish, and they would irrevocably fall into the Assyrian snare (vs. 13).[a]

However, had they heeded the prophet's warning and obeyed the word of God, they would have been delivered (vs. 12a). Then, instead of the *"strange lips and alien tongue"* of the Assyrians being a sign of judgment, they would have been a sign of God's mercy and protection. The Lord would have driven the enemy far away and brought prosperity to his people.

(2) An analogy with glossolalia

Paul saw in that ancient oracle a picture of the effect of glossolalia in the church and on the unbeliever. Apparently the Corinthians were trying to use glossolalia to convince and convert unbelievers. He condemns that practice, and shows that *"strange tongues"* will have the same effect on unbelievers today as did the *"strange tongues"* of old. Far from convincing the ungodly, the opposite will occur: *"they will not listen to me, says the Lord"* (1 Co 14:21); *"they will say that you are mad"* (vs. 23). That was just the reaction of the onlookers on the day of Pentecost (Ac 2:12-13). The situation there was retrieved

---

[a] Notice though 33:19 & 59:21, where the Lord promises to deliver them from the foreign tongue and to put his Spirit upon them. Then their mouths would be filled with His own words (glossolalia?), which would continue generation after generation until the time of the end.

only because God wrought a special miracle by causing the tongues to be understood (vs. 6-8).

Glossolalia then, to unbelievers, is a stumbling block that causes them to fall away from God; it becomes to them a sign of divine judgment - just as the *"alien tongue"* of the Assyrians was a sign of heaven's anger in the time of Isaiah. When Paul says that *"tongues are a sign ... for unbelievers"*, he means it in the negative. They are a sign only in the sense of sealing unbelievers in their unbelief, and of condemning them to judgment.

In scripture some signs are given to *convince*, others to *condemn*, and still others to serve *both* functions. For example, the wonders Moses wrought *condemned* Egypt, but *convinced* Israel of their calling in God. So glossolalia may be "good" for the believer; but to an unbeliever it may act as a condemnatory sign, hardening unbelief. It is futile to expect that glossolalia, by itself, will draw unbelievers to God; it will tend rather to drive them away

Does this mean that all speaking in tongues must stop if an unbeliever comes into a church meeting? Hardly. Paul himself did not require such drastic action (vs. 26-28). He means only that glossolalia *by itself* will bring no life to an unbeliever. On the contrary, *"if the whole church has assembled, and everyone is (doing nothing else except) speak in tongues"*, unbelievers will rightly reckon it a congregation of imbeciles. But the reverse is also true:

- ♦ if glossolalia is exercised in an orderly fashion, and
- ♦ if a prophetic tongue is followed by interpretation, and
- ♦ if glossolalia is associated with the preaching of the Word of God, and
- ♦ if due place is also given to *"hymns, lessons, revelations"* and so on, then

the unbeliever may well be won for Christ - and glossolalia will play a part in winning him. Those things are comprehended in the saying,

> *"if everyone prophesies, and unbelievers or outsiders enter, the words of the whole congregation will bring them under conviction; they will be called to account for their sin, the secrets of their hearts will be revealed, and falling on their faces, they will worship God and declare that God is really among you!" (vs. 24)*

I take it that Paul uses the phrase *"if all prophecy"* in a general sense. He can hardly mean it in the strict sense of "the spiritual gift of prophecy," because that gift is limited to two or three speakers in any one meeting (vs. 29). By "prophecy" (in vs. 24) he must mean simply the Spirit-quickened proclamation of the Word of God by the entire congregation through hymns, psalms, lessons, sermons, prayers, the gift of prophecy, the gift of tongues/interpretation, other charismatic gifts, and so on.

In other words, a true Pentecostal worship service should have about it a prophetic character; it should be overshadowed by a mantle of prophecy. There you should find the people of God witnessing to the presence of God among them, and declaring his Word, by the power of the Holy Spirit who is working in every part of their worship.

(3) Demarcation and Rest

In Isaiah's day the witness of the Assyrian tongue had a two-fold effect:

- ◆ *first:* it created a line of demarcation, an insurmountable barrier, between the godly and the ungodly in Israel (Is 28:14-16); and
- ◆ *second:* it signified the wrath of God against the unrighteous, and the salvation and comfort of God for the righteous (vs. 12).

Glossolalia today has the same effect. For those whose hearts are open toward God, who receive his heavenly gift, it holds a promise of sweet *"rest and repose"*. In this sense glossolalia creates a sharp division between those who are within the church and those who are without. It is a sign to the unbeliever that he is indeed an *"outsider"*. It is equally a sign to the believer that he is indeed a *"believer"*, in the full sense in which Christ probably used the word (Mk 16:17,20).

Again, Isaiah promised the people of his day that God would give them *"rest and repose"*. They had only to heed the witness of the *"alien tongue"* through which he was speaking to them. But they would not hear, and they perished. There are many who still will not hear. But to us who *have* heard, and who still gladly hear *"the strange tongues"* through which God speaks to us, the word of the prophet has been proved blessedly true. To pray, to sing, to bless God, to speak mysteries in the spirit - these things truly do bring rest to our souls, sweet repose to our spirits, delightful refreshment to our minds, and life to our entire being! Blessed river of living water! For this, O God, we thank you!

Chapter Twelve

SPIRITUAL PRAYER

If you have purchased or read *Clothed With Power*, the companion volume to this one, I hope you will not be too annoyed when you find that this chapter echoes some of its pages. However, the ideas expressed here seem to me to be so important, and because some may read one book, but not the other, I decided to include them in both books.

> *"Those who speak in a tongue are not speaking to people, but to God ... (for) they are uttering mysteries in the spirit ... If I pray in a tongue, my spirit is praying ... I will pray with the spirit ... I will sing with the spirit ... I will bless with the spirit" (1 Co 14:2,14-16).*

The Greek word *"pneuma"* (spirit) should be translated in each of those places without an initial capital, for the reference is not to the **Holy** Spirit, but to the **human** spirit. Glossolalia is not an activity of the Spirit of God, but of the human spirit. *I* speak in tongues, not God. The utterance comes directly from *my* spirit, and arises only indirectly from the Spirit of God. Paul's statements here, and the sharp contrast he draws between *"praying with the spirit"* and *"praying with the mind"*, lead to some fascinating ideas which I now want to explore with you.

(A) GLOSSOLALIA RELEASED BY THE HOLY SPIRIT

Holy Spirit baptism is the catalyst that releases the phenomenon of glossolalia in the believer (Ac 2:4). But how does this occur? And how does the gift remain with the believer, to be exercised at will, in love or without love, blessedly or basely? I suggest that just as the human *mind* possesses an inherent ability to express itself through a known language, so the human *spirit* possesses an inherent ability to express itself through an unknown language.

The vocal ability of the mind is released by education; but the vocal ability of the spirit requires a very different catalyst. In the case of a Christian that catalyst is Holy Spirit baptism. So the ability to express itself in glossolalia may be said to be natural to the human spirit, but it lies dormant until released by the Holy Spirit. Hence glossolalia is supernatural only in that it has a supernatural origin; thereafter it becomes a natural function of the human spirit.

This is demonstrated by the way in which Paul places *"prayer with the spirit"* alongside of *"prayer with the mind."* He shows two things:

- ♦ *contrast,* in that one is rational, the other irrational; one is intelligible the other unintelligible.

But there is also

- ♦ *congruence*, in that both are wholly under the person's volitional control.

Paul says that just as, with his mind, he can pray in the vernacular, so, with his spirit, he can pray in glossolalia. Both functions are natural to him and equally subject to his control. To pray with the spirit requires only what is needed to pray with the mind: an act of will. He asks, *"what am I to do?"* And he answers, *"I will pray with the spirit, and I will pray with the mind!"* Notice the words, *"I will!"* It requires no more effort, nor any different circumstances, for him to pray with the spirit than to pray with the mind. It was simply a matter of which form of prayer he chose to employ at any given time; and he apparently made equal use of both forms.

Yet not only the *time* or *place* in which he exercised glossolalia was under his control, but also the manner (cp. vs. 32). Whatever he could do in the vernacular, he could obviously do in glossolalia also. He could pray in tongues or sing, bless God or give thanks. He could speak softly or loudly, with or without love, with joy, sorrow, or with no emotion at all. By inference, it is plain that he could also, if he chose, rail against God in glossolalia. So it appears that the ability to speak in tongues, once it has been released in the human spirit, remains until death. It is there permanently, and may be used at any time and in any way, with or without the influence of the Holy Spirit.

(B) SOME NECESSARY CONCLUSIONS

If it is true that glossolalia remains a natural function of the human spirit, once it has been released by Holy Spirit baptism, then certain conclusions follow -

(1) It is erroneous to think that glossolalia is an involuntary phenomenon, that a person can speak in tongues only when under a powerful emotional or spiritual impulsion. Even in its initial occurrence, in association with Holy Spirit baptism, the Spirit does not speak in tongues, we do. The Spirit imparts the utterance; but once imparted, it remains wholly under the recipient's volition - and it can be exercised in cooperation with, or in opposition to, the Spirit. The choice is ours.

(2) Since one of the fruits of Spirit is *"self-control"* (Ga 5:23), it is unreasonable to suppose that he will impart to us a gift that involves the loss of self-control! On the contrary, the Christian should never be more in control of himself, never more aware of himself, never stronger, than when he or she is filled with the Spirit of God. It is surely nonsense to suppose that God wants nothing so much as to reduce his servants to a state of mental, spiritual, or physical catalepsy. The baptism in the Spirit is not a spiritual narcotic, drugging believers into a state of comatose bliss. God does not make us marionettes dancing to the tug of a heavenly string. Those characteristics are the mark of heathen religions, and of demon spirits.[a]

Against such pagan ideas stands the gospel, which teaches that God reaches out to men and women to ennoble them, not debase them. He seeks to enhance human dignity, not destroy it; to restore our personhood, not ruin it; to give us true self-awareness and self-control, not to obliterate our identity nor to enslave us. If I could speak in tongues only at the cost of falling into an ecstatic trance, of surrendering my own volition, of being seized by a corybantic frenzy, then I would fiercely reject glossolalia as an enemy of the gospel.

Fortunately, the opposite is true! I have not found that the gifts of the Spirit require me to lose personal identity, to become a machine, an automaton. On the contrary, the presence of those gifts reinforces my integrity as a person made in the image of God. They strengthen my inviolability as a free moral agent. They enable me to better realise myself as a unique individual, and to fulfil better all the potential that is in me. They assist me to stand as a true man, fully self-aware, fully self-controlled.

If the charismata are genuinely from God, then they will always have the effect of more sharply delineating each Christian's special personhood, and of enabling them to stand taller as free children of God. To do otherwise would violate the gospel.

(3) So the controlling factor in the exercise of glossolalia, or any of the charismata, is not just a feeling of emotional or spiritual compulsion, nor any other kind of manic urge. The charismata should be controlled by *the human will*. These gifts must be exercised within a framework of enlightened and sanctified responsibility. They are not quaint baubles given to amuse the spiritually and emotionally immature. They are serious gifts, given for a serious purpose (albeit

---

[a] See again the Addendum at the end of Chapter One

filled with joy), and this purpose will be realised only when those who use the charismata bring themselves and their gifts under the rule of scripture, and when they acknowledge that the spirit of each person must always remain subject to the control of the mind.

(4) Since glossolalia, once received, remains a natural function of the human spirit, the ability to speak in tongues will continue even if the person backslides. Paul shows this when he writes, *"I may speak with the tongues of men and angels; but if I lack love then I am nothing but a noisy gong, a clanging cymbal"* (1 Co 13:1). A carnal person speaking in other tongues makes the gift wholly natural, a mere clatter of sounds, void of any divine grace.

Note how Paul lists several charismata that can be exercised without love (vs. 1-3, *tongues, prophecy, word of wisdom, word of knowledge, faith, working of miracles*). Of them all, glossolalia is the only one that completely fails in effectiveness. Why? Because glossolalia (with the possible inclusion of prophecy and interpretation) is the one gift that can be entirely exercised from the human spirit without any help from the Holy Spirit.

Even if the Holy Spirit were to depart altogether from a backslidden Christian, his or her ability to speak in tongues would remain. But, of course, without the directing influence of the Holy Spirit the human spirit must soon lapse into carnality. Whatever prophetic gifts that person once had will be emptied of divine significance.

(5) It seems that glossolalia spoken without love becomes just as unintelligible to God as it ordinarily is to human ears. The human mind is always *"unfruitful"* in the presence of glossolalia; and the Divine mind will be equally unfruitful unless, by the addition of love and the enlivening touch of the Holy Spirit, the utterance becomes impregnated with meaning.

(6) So, to become truly supernatural, and to achieve its divinely ordained purpose, glossolalia must be exercised in *conscious union* with the Holy Spirit. It is not enough merely to speak in tongues. The person who does that may be doing nothing except make an

unpleasant noise. To the ear of God it will be an offensive and jangling cacophony. Instead, all who speak in tongues should yield themselves to the Holy Spirit; they should pour out their hearts in worship and praise to God; they should speak with sincere love. When that is done, then glossolalia gains nuances and cadences that gladden the Father and bring to each worshipper a rich and reciprocal edification.

(7) There is a parallel here to prophecy. My vernacular speech is English, a language in which I can speak either *naturally or supernaturally*. When my words are governed solely by my own mind, without reference to the Holy Spirit, they are quite natural, and may even be sinful. But when I yield myself to the Holy Spirit, and in his anointing, under his guidance, speak to the church in prophecy, then my English words become supernatural. The church knows the difference between words that are the product of my own mind, and the message that comes from the Spirit, rich with heaven's grace and powerful in heaven's unction!

So I can speak both naturally and supernaturally with my mind; and much the same is true of speaking with my spirit. The major difference is that most of my vernacular speech must necessarily be natural, with only occasional forays into the supernatural; but *all* glossolalic speech should be touched by the supernatural or it will be as meaningless as the banging of a drunken drummer. [a]

(8) From what I have been saying it should be obvious that I consider glossolalia to be normally unintelligible. Not only is it incomprehensible to those who are present, but it would normally be incomprehensible to any person anywhere. While there are occasions when glossolalia will consist of a known language (e.g. as on the day

---

[a] I have watched a formerly Spirit-filled person roll on the floor backslidden and blind-drunk, slurring away in tongues. I wonder what it sounded like to God? It repulsed me.

of Pentecost), in ordinary usage glossolalia does not consist of any known language. [a]

Now the suggestion that glossolalia has no intelligent or rational base, that it does not consist of any known language, is startling to some people. They feel that this reduces glossolalia to mere gibberish. But it can be called gibberish only if it is evaluated on the basis of criteria that are proper only for ordinary language. But glossolalia is the language of the *spirit*, not of the mind. It is not addressed to man; it does not have to appeal to the mind; in fact, Paul says that the mind, in the presence of glossolalia, is *"unfruitful"* and that *"no one can understand it"* (1 Co 14:2,14,16-17). Since it is the language of the spirit why insist that glossolalia must have logical structure? Intelligibility can be demanded only of that which must address its appeal to the mind. But that is the very thing glossolalia does not do!

Furthermore, if glossolalia were subject to the laws that bind ordinary language; if, when I spoke in tongues, I had to be speaking one of the native languages of earth, what have I gained? In what way have I improved my prayer life? I already have a fair command of one of the world's richest and most expressive languages (English), and whatever the human mind can say I am already able to say. Yet there are many things my mind cannot say, many deep and wondrous things for which logical language is just not adequate. There are things I want to say that I could not say, even if I knew every word in every language in the world. That is the anguish of poetry (and often of prayer), that people sense beauty, mystery, and wonder that they struggle to put into words; yet perfection of expression always eludes them. Behind all great poetry (as also in art and music) there is always a haunting feeling that while the poet has said more than any

---

[a] If someone draws my attention to Paul's "tongues of men", I point to his next phrase, "and of angels"! Both expressions are hyperbolic descriptions of glossolalia.

other man, there is so much more that evaded his grasp, so much mystery his words could not capture.

I do not believe that when I speak in tongues I am only speaking Greek, or Swahili, or Chinese, so that my prayer is bound by the limitations that restrict the expressive powers of all human language. Glossolalia is free of all such restraints. it is the soaring language of the spirit! It is not bound by formal rules of logic and grammar! Such things are needed by men, but not by God! I rejoice that in my weakness of speech I can turn to the Holy Spirit, and know that he will intercede for me, through me, with language and sighs too deep for ordinary words! (Ro 8:26-27).

(9) Philologists and linguists have often criticised the lack in glossolalia of those structural features that usually characterise a valid language. Whether the observations of those experts are correct or not, I wouldn't know; nonetheless I would actually expect glossolalia to defy logical analysis. The lack of any discernible structure, far from invalidating glossolalia and reducing it to meaningless sounds, simply confirms its nature as a spiritual language. As such, it does not require a meaning or a pattern intelligible to the mind. God receives glossolalia, not as a succession of meaningful words, but as the fragrance of a rose, total in itself, expressing beauty and love; or as an unbroken light, in one beam searching and exposing those things that are hidden; or as a beautiful symphony, a soaring paean of praise. Just as rapture seizes my soul when I gaze at a magnificent sunset, or wonder about the mystery of an evening silhouette, or stand surrounded by the dazzling terror of a shattering thunder storm, so the Father finds joy when that stream of living water pours from my innermost being and climbs to the very throne of heaven, and there moves him with an undying melody of love.

BIBLIOGRAPHY

Against Heresies; Church Fathers; In loc.

Believer's Bible Commentary; William Macdonald; Thomas Nelson Publishers; 1989.

Bible Background Commentary; Intervarsity Press, Nottingham UK; 1993.

Bible Knowledge Commentary, The; by John Walvoord and Roy Zuck; Cook Communications, Colorado Springs, Colorado; 1989.

Calvin's Commentaries; John Calvin (1509-1564).

City of God, The; St. Augustine of Hippo; Penguin Books Ltd.; Harmondsworth, Middlesex, England, Reprinted 1976.

College Press NIV Commentary, The; Joplin, Missouri; 1996.

Commentary on Ephesians, A; Charles Hodge (1797-1878).

Commentary on the Bible; Adam Clarke (1715-1832).

Commentary On The Old And New Testaments, A; John Trapp (1601-1669).

Commentary on the Old and New Testaments, A; Robert Jamieson, A. R. Fausset, David Brown; 1871.

Explanatory Notes on the Whole Bible; John Wesley (1703-1791).

Exposition of the Entire Bible; John Gill (1690-1771).

Expositor's Bible Commentary, The; ed. Frank E. Gaebelein; Zondervan Publishers, Grand Rapids, Michigan.

Expository Commentary; H.A. Ironside (1876-1951).

Holman New Testament Commentary; ed. Max Anders; B & H Publishing Group, Nashville, Tennessee; 2004.

Interpreter's Bible, The; Abingdon Press, New York; 1952.

IVP New Testament Commentary Series, The; Intervarsity Press, Nottingham, UK.

Jewish New Testament Commentary; David H. Stern; Jewish New Testament Publications, Inc., Clarksville, Maryland; 1982.

Maccabees; The Apocrypha

Matthew Henry's Commentary; Marshall, Morgan, and Scott, London; 1953.

Matthew Poole's Commentary; 1685

Nelson's New Illustrated Bible Commentary; Thomas Nelson Inc., New York; 1999.

New Testament Commentary; Baker's Publishing House, Grand Rapids, Michigan; 1987.

Notes on the Bible; Albert Barnes (1798-1870).

People's New Testament Commentary, The; B. W. Johnson; Word Search Corporation, Nashville, Tennessee; 2010.

People's New Testament, The; by B. W. Johnson; 1891.

Poor Man's Commentary On The Whole Bible, The; Robert Hawker; 1850.

Preacher's Commentary, The; Word Inc., Nashville, Tennessee; 1992.

Preacher's Outline and Sermon Bible; Word Search Corporation, Nashville, Tennessee; 2010.

Pulpit Commentary, The; ed. Joseph S. Exell, Henry Donald Maurice Spence-Jones; 1881.

Treasury of David, The; compiled by C. H. Spurgeon; Zondervan Publishing; Grand Rapids, Michigan; 1974.

Vincent's Word Studies; Marvin R. Vincent; 1886

Wiersbe's Expository Outlines; Warren W. Wiersbe; Publisher, David C. Cook, Colorado Springs, Colorado.

Word Pictures In The New Testament; A. T. Robertson; 1933.

www.ingramcontent.com/pod-product-compliance
Lightning Source LLC
Chambersburg PA
CBHW052010090426

42741CB00008B/1628